GOD Healed Me
HE Will Heal YOU

48 Testimonies on Healing

Dr Michael H Yeager

All rights reserved. No part of this book is allowed to be reproduced, stored in a retrieval system, or transmitted by any form or by any means-electronic, mechanical, photocopy, recording, or otherwise-without prior written permission of the copyright owner, except by a reviewer who wishes to quote brief passages in connection with a review for inclusion in a magazine, website, newspaper, podcast, or broadcast. All Scripture quotations, unless otherwise indicated, are taken from the King James Authorized Version of the Bible.

(Some of the teaching in this book is partly taken from the Adam Clarke Commentary, and other non-copy right material found on the internet)

Copyright © 2017 Dr Michael H Yeager

All rights reserved.

ISBN: 1981135812
ISBN-13: 9781981135813

DEDICATION

All of the Scriptures used in this book on **"GOD Healed Me HE Will Heal YOU"** is from the original 1611 version of the King James Bible. I give thanks to God the Father , Jesus Christ and the Holy Ghost for the powerful impact the word has had upon my life. Without the word Quickened in my heart by the Holy Ghost I would've been lost and undone. To the Lord of Heaven and Earth I am eternally indebted for his great love and his mercy, his protections and his provisions, his divine guidance and overwhelming goodness, the **Price He PAID for my Healing**! To him be glory and praise for ever and ever: Amen .

CONTENTS

	Acknowledgments	i
1	Chapter One	1
2	Chapter Two	13
3	Chapter Three	24
4	Chapter Four	33
5	Chapter Five	43
6	Chapter Six	54
7	Chapter Seven	64
8	Chapter Eight	71
9	Chapter Nine	87
10	Chapter Ten	95

ACKNOWLEDGMENTS

*To our heavenly Father and His wonderful love.

*To our Lord, Savior and Master — Jesus Christ, Who saved us and set us free because of His great love for us.

*To the Holy Spirit, Who leads and guides us into the realm of truth and miraculous living every day.

*To all of those who had a part in helping me get this book ready for the publishers.

*To my Lovely Wife, and our precious children, Michael, Daniel, Steven, Stephanie, Catherine Yu, who is our precious daughter-in-law, and Naomi, who is now with the Lord.

"GOD Healed Me HE Will Heal YOU"

Important Introduction

The **HEALING'S** I have seen, experienced, and share in this book are all true. They have happened personally to me, my family and others. These healings are recalled and shared to the best of my ability.

By no means do the following stories account for all the healings and miracles that we have seen, and experienced in my live. If we would recount every single answer to prayer, and every wonderful healing, miracle and blessing, there would be no end to this book!

What I am about to share with you in this book are simply some highlights of what we have experienced in the Lord. Some of these experiences will seem to be incredulous, however, they are true. This is not a testimony of how spiritual we are, but how wonderful and marvelous the Father, the Son, and the Holy Ghost are! I share these experiences to the best of my recollections and understanding. Not every conversation I share in these experiences are exactly word for word. I would love to name every person that was a part of these wonderful occurrences, but privacy laws do not allow this. If you are reading this book and you saw, experienced, or were a part of these events, please do not be offended because your names were not mentioned.

Dr Michael H Yeager

CHAPTER ONE

What authority Do I Have when it comes to **Healing**? You see I have been **HEALED** of at least **20** major ailments and afflictions. This without the use of medicine or the doctors!(I am not against doctors or medicine)

#1, Healed of major allergies
#2, Healed of loss of the sense of smell
#3, Healed of birth defects in the bones of my ears
#4, Healed of a speech impediment
#5, Healed of a broken back
#6, Healed of burned out vocal cords
#7, I was raised from the dead by my wife
#8 Healed of painful tumors in my abdomen
#9 Healed of a serious hernia
#10, Healed of a broken crushed kneecap
#11, Healed of dangerous attack of conjunctivitis
#12, Healed of arthritis
#13, Healed instantly of a broken busted foot
#14, My son Healed from rabies
#15, Healed from prostate cancer
#16, Healed from life-threatening colon cancer
#17, Healed instantly of a broken twisted index finger
#18, Healed overnight of second-degree Burns
#19, Healed of gushing bright red blood
#20, Many Healings, on daily basis since Feb 18, 1975.

PLEASE UNDERSTAND I AM BRAGGING ABOUT JESUS!

What God has done for me, he will do for you! He is not a respecter of people. As you read these testimonies, and the truths revealed within them, May faith rise up in your heart to be Healed!

Acts 10:34 Then Peter opened his mouth, and said, Of a truth I perceive that God is no respecter of persons:

Romans 2:11 For there is no respect of persons with God.

#1 Why God heals me Time. (1975)

While reading my Bible as a brand new believer, (1975) I discovered that Jesus Christ went about healing **ALL** who were sick and oppressed of the devil. I began to search the Scriptures on this particular subject, and as I studied I discovered many Scriptures that support this:

Surely he hath borne our griefs, and carried our sorrows: yet we did esteem him stricken, smitten of God, and afflicted. But he was wounded for our transgressions, he was bruised for our iniquities: the chastisement of our peace was upon him; and with his stripes we are healed (Isaiah 53:4-5).

Who his own self bare our sins in his own body on the tree, that we, being dead to sins, should live unto righteousness: by whose stripes ye were healed.1 Peter 2:24

When the even was come, they brought unto him many

"GOD Healed Me HE Will Heal YOU"

that were possessed with devils: and he cast out the spirits with his word, and healed all that were sick: That it might be fulfilled which was spoken by Esaias the prophet, saying, Himself took our infirmities, and bare our sicknesses. Matthew 8:16-17

As I read and meditated upon these Scriptures, something wonderful happened within my heart. Great, overwhelming sorrow took a hold of me as I saw the pain and the agony that Jesus went through for my healing. In my heart and in my mind I saw that Jesus had taken my sicknesses and my diseases. I then experienced a great love for the son of God, and recognize the price he paid for my healing. When God gave me this revelation, revealed to me by the Scriptures, I experienced a great an overwhelming love for the son of God, recognizing the price he had paid for my healing.

It was like an open vision in which I saw my precious **Lord and Savior** tied to the whipping post. I saw the Roman soldiers striking, beating, and whipping the back of Jesus with the cat of nine tails. This was a Roman whip which had nine long strands, coated with oil, and covered with glass, metal shards, and sharp objects. In this vision I saw the flesh and the blood of my precious Savior splashing everything within a 10-foot radius, with each terrible stroke of the Romans soldier's whip hitting his body.

As I saw this open vision, (as I was on my knees in prayer) I wept because I knew that this horrendous beating he was enduring was for my healing, and my deliverance. To this day, even after 40 years, whenever I retell this story, great love, and sorrow still fills my heart for what Christ had to endure for me. This is the reason why I am so aggressive in my fight to receive healing. Still I have great joy, wonderful peace, and enthusiasm in this battle, because I know that by the **stripes of Jesus Christ I am healed**. This amazing price that he paid (God in the flesh) was not only for me, but for every believer who has received Christ as their Lord and Savior.

In this moment of this vision something exploded within my heart, an amazing faith possessed me with the knowledge that I no longer have to be sick. In the name of Jesus for over 40 years I have refused to allow what my precious Lord went through to be for nothing. I have refused to allow sickness and disease to dwell in my body, which is the temple of the Holy Ghost.

Jesus has taken my sicknesses and my diseases. No if, an, or butts, no matter what it looks like or how I feel, I know within my heart Jesus Christ has set me free from sicknesses and diseases. At the moment of this revelation great anger, yes great anger, rose up in my heart against the enemy of my Lord. The demonic world has no right to afflict me or any other believer, because Jesus took our sicknesses and bore our diseases.

Now I had been born with terrible physical infirmities, but now I found myself speaking out loud with authority to my ears, commanding them to be open and to be normal in the name of Jesus Christ of Nazareth. Then I spoke to my lungs, and commanded them to be healed in the name of Jesus Christ of Nazareth. Next I commanded my sinuses to be delivered, so I could smell normal scents in the name of Jesus Christ of Nazareth.

The minute I spoke the Word of God to my physical man, my ears popped completely open. Up to this moment I had a significant hearing loss, but now as I was listening to Christian music playing softly (at least I thought it was) the music became so loud that I had to turn it down. My lungs were clear, and I haven't experienced any lung congestion since in 40 years. I used to be so allergic to dust that my mother had to work extra hard to keep our house dust-free. I would literally end up in an oxygen tent in the hospital. From that moment to now dust, allergies, mold, or any such thing have never come back to torment me or cause me problems. Instantly my sense of smell returned! I had broken my nose about four times due to fights, accidents, and rough activities. I could barely smell anything.

Suddenly, I could smell a terrible odor. I tried to find out where it was coming from and then I looked at my feet and wondered if it could be them. I put my foot on a night stand and bent over toward it. I took a big sniff and nearly fell over. Man, did my feet stink! I went straight over to the bathroom and washed

"GOD Healed Me HE Will Heal YOU"

them in the sink.

The very 1st thing we must do to build a solid foundation for our lives is to let go of all our traditions, philosophies, doctrines, and experiences that contradict what is revealed to us through Jesus Christ. We must go back to Matthew, Mark, Luke and John rediscovering who Jesus Christ really is. Whatever Jesus said and did is what we agree with wholeheartedly. Any voice or teaching that contradicts Christ, and his redemptive work I immediately reject.

#2 God Raised Kimberly from the Bed of Death 11/15/2017

Right after I dropped the men off who have been working at our church community service, I received a phone call. I was driving the van back to our church facility. The phone call was from Sandra. I had to ask her to repeat herself because she was crying and she was so upset.

I asked her what was wrong? She informed me that her oldest daughter (56) Kimberly was at the Chambersburg Hospital. She informed me that the doctors told her they had no hope for her to make it through the night. That all of her vital signs had plummeted. That she was leaking blood and he did not know exactly where. That her bowels also had an obstruction somewhere. They told her they were simply trying to make her comfortable until her passing.

I told her that I would be right there, and not to give up hope. As I drove the van back to the church I began to pray to the Heavenly Father. I began to take authority over this spirit of death and infirmity commanding it to go. I kept declaring she would live and not die. You see I do all my praying before I ever go to lay hands on a person.

I got back to the church's parsonage, and went in and change my clothes. I informed my children what was going on for they could agree with me. Then I got in my wife's Toyota, Prius.

(Kathleen is with her mother right now in Altoona hospital) As I drove the vehicle towards Chambersburg I kept on boldly proclaiming "In Jesus Name Shall Live and Not Die". I began to quote John 15 were declares - "If We Abide in Christ, and He Abides in Us, We Can Ask What We Will, and It Will Be Done unto Us"

What I am about to say will sound presumptuous, but it's not. I knew in my heart that she would live and not die. You see I have been abiding in Christ and his word has been abiding in me. The Scripture says that we can have confidence that if we are praying according to his will, and we are abiding in his will and his word, God will hear us when we pray.

I finally arrived at the hospital and headed to the CCU. When I walked into Kimberly's hospital room you could tell there was a real heaviness of fear and sorrow. There was a nurse who was actively busy trying to make sure Kimberly was comfortable.

Sandra was there with her husband Ted who is also a member of our church. There one daughter who had not met yet was there Carol. They said there youngest daughter Kathy was on her way. Sandra informed me of what was happening to her daughter at that moment.

I informed them that we were going to lay our hands upon Kimberly and that she would live and not die. This is not me speaking, but the spirit of God that was rising up within me. You do not have to pray any real loud prayers. You must reach heaven before you ever pray, with the laying on of hands.

I encouraged Sandra, and Ted and Carol to lay hands on Kimberly. Where they had placed an IV into Kimberly's shoulder there was lots of blood. The nurse said they could not get the blood to stop flowing. We **laid hands** on Kimberly and I simply spoke the word of God. We commanded her vital signs to come back. We **commanded** the blood to stop flowing and to be normal. We **commanded** the obstruction in her bowels to be gone. We **commanded** her to live and not die!

"GOD Healed Me HE Will Heal YOU"

Mark 16:17 And these signs shall follow them that believe; In my name shall they cast out devils; ......18 ...... they shall lay hands on the sick, and they shall recover.19 So then after that Jesus had spoken unto them, he was received up into heaven, and sat on the right hand of God.

This prayer probably lasted less than a minute. Then we stepped back, and I encourage them just trust God. During this whole time, Kimberly was able to communicate with us. We'd stood there for a while just talking when their youngest daughter Kathy came into the room. She gave us all a big hug with tears in her eyes, and I informed her that everything was going to be okay. I do not speak these kinds of words just out of my mind or my emotions. It rises up in my innermost being.

When I knew my heart that my time was there was done, I said goodbye to everybody and informed them that I will continue to believe God. And then I headed back home because it had been a long day.

GOOD REPORT!

Sandra just called me to inform me that her daughter was going to live and not die. That all of her vital signs had come back to normal. The stats had been way off the chart, but now they were normal. Thank you, Jesus! The blood had started clotting on his own. They are not getting ready to take her into examine where the obstruction to the bow was. Already the doctors are talking like as if it just disappeared on its own. God still answers prayer, all we have to do is be aggressive, use our authority, speak the word, and trust God. Then we just keep praising Jesus no matter how it looks! God will always come through if we will just simply believe him.

#3 My Mom's Hip Miraculously Healed (1975)

I was visiting my parent's home in Wisconsin. One day when I came home, my mother asked me to help her get her hip back into place where it belonged. For some reason her right hip would pop out of place which was extremely painful and difficult for her. When this happened she would lay on the floor and grab onto something heavy and solid like the china hutch or the dining room table leg. Next, she would have one of us four boys grab her right ankle and pull with all our might with a heavy jerk until her hip would go back into place. She was just a little lady, so when we pulled her leg it would pull her whole body off the floor.

I told my mother I would help her. She laid down on her back on the dining room floor and grabbed the dining room table leg. I knelt down on my knees and took a hold of her right ankle with both hands. She was waiting for me to jerk her leg with a powerful pull but Instead of pulling like I normally would, I whispered: "In the name of Jesus Christ of Nazareth I command this hip to go back into place."

The minute I whispered this a wonderful miracle transpired. Her leg instantly shot straight out. She was very surprised asked with a shocked voice, "Michael, what did you just do to me?" I told her what I had done. Then I shared the reality of Jesus with her. As far as I know until she went home to be with the Lord, for the next 25 years she never had another problem with that hip popping out of its socket.

And these signs shall follow them that believe; In my name shall they cast out devils; they shall speak with new tongues; They shall take up serpents; and if they drink any deadly thing, it shall not hurt them; they shall lay hands on the sick, and they shall recover (Mark 16:17-18)

"GOD Healed Me HE Will Heal YOU"

#4 A Preacher's Son Was Dying (1977)

One night I was fishing for souls in front of the old movie theater in Mount Union PA. Out of the darkness came the son of an African American minister I knew. I knew this minister's son was in a backslidden condition and was involved in heavy drugs and alcohol. The world had swallowed him up!

And here he was coming toward me. I could tell something drastic was wrong with him as he approached me. He was barely able to stand on his feet. He said, "Mike, help me. I'm dying." He had evidently gotten some bad drugs and asked if I would please pray and ask God to do a miracle and save him. I took him into the restroom on the second floor of that old movie theater, laid my hands upon him, and cried out to Jesus for mercy—that He would remove the drugs from his bloodstream.

I commanded the poisons, drugs, and alcohol to come out of his body right then in the name of Jesus Christ! The very minute I finished praying it was as if God snapped His fingers. All of the chemicals and drugs came out of him instantly and he stood straight up. One minute he was a goner and the next minute he was absolutely straight, sober and healed. The preacher's son was completely mystified and told me that all the symptoms and effects of the drugs were completely gone.

#5 My Broken Back Healed (1977)

I share these stories, my personal experiences, hoping that they will give you an insight in how to receive healing, even in the most difficult situations. Now in the winter of 1977, I was working at the Belleville Feed & Grain Mill. My job was to pick up the corn, wheat, and oats from the farmers, and bring it to the mill.

There it would be mixed and combined with other products for the farmers' livestock.

One cold, snowy day, the owner of the feed mill told me to deliver a load of cattle feed to an Amish farm. It was an extremely bad winter that year, with lots of snow. I was driving an International 1600 Lodestar. I backed up as far as I could to this Amish man's barn without getting stuck. The Amish never had their lanes plowed in those days, and they most likely still do not. I was approximately seventy-five feet away from his barn, which meant that I had to carry the bags at least seventy-five feet. I think there were about eighty bags of feed, with each bag weighing approximately one hundred pounds. During those years I only weighed about 130 pounds.

I would carry one bag on each of my shoulders, stumbling and pushing my way through the heavy, deep snow to get up the steep incline into the barn. Then I would stack the bags in a dry location. As usual, nobody came out to help me. Many a time when delivering things to the farms, the Amish would watch me work without lending a helping hand. About the third trip, something frightening happened to me as I was carrying two one-hundred-pound bags upon my shoulders. I felt the bones in my back snap. Something drastic just happened. I fell to the ground at that very moment almost completely crippled. I could barely move. I was filled with intense overwhelming pain.

I had been spending a lot of my time meditating in the Word of God. Every morning, I would get up about 5:00 a.m. to study. I had one of those little bread baskets with memorization scriptures in it. I believe you can still buy them to this day at a Christian bookstore. Every morning I would memorize from three to five of them. It would not take me very long, so all day long I would be meditating on these verses.

The very minute I fell down, immediately I cried out to Jesus, asking him to forgive me for my pride, and for being so stupid in carrying two hundred pounds on my little frame. After I asked Jesus to forgive me, I commanded my back to be healed in the

"GOD Healed Me HE Will Heal YOU"

name of Jesus Christ of Nazareth. Since I believed I was healed, I knew that I had to act now upon my faith. Please understand that I was full of tremendous pain, but I had declared that I was healed by the stripes of Jesus. The Word of God came out of my mouth as I tried to get up and then fell back down.

Even though the pain was more intense than I can express, I kept getting back up speaking the name of Jesus, then I would fall back down again. I fell down more times than I can remember. After some time, I was able to take a couple steps, then I would fall again. This entire time I was saying, "In the name of Jesus, in the name of Jesus, in the name of Jesus." I finally was able to get to the truck. I said to myself if I believe I'm healed then I will unload this truck in the name of Jesus. Of course, I did not have a cell phone in order to call for help and the Amish did not own any phones on their property. Now, even if they would have had a phone, I would not have called for help. I had already called upon my help, and His name was Jesus Christ. I knew in my heart that by the stripes of Jesus I was healed. I then pulled a bag off of the back of the truck, with it falling on top of me. I would drag it a couple feet, and then fall down.

Tears were running down my face as I spoke the Word of God over and over. By the time I was done with all of the bags, the sun had already gone down. Maybe six or seven hours had gone by. I painstakingly pulled myself up into that big old 1600 Lodestar. It took everything within me to shift gears, pushing in the clutch, and driving it. I had to sit straight like a board all the way.

I finally got back to the feed mill late in the evening. Everybody had left for home a long time ago with the building being locked up. I struggled out of the Lodestar and stumbled and staggered over to my Ford pickup. I got into my pickup, and made it back to the converted chicken house. I went back to my cold, unheated, plywood floor room. It took everything in me to get my clothes off. It was a very rough and long night.

The next morning when I woke up, I was so stiff that I could not bend in the least. I was like a board. Of course, I was not going to miss work, because by the stripes of Jesus I was healed. In order to get out of bed, I had to literally roll off the bed, hitting the floor. Once I had hit the floor, it took everything for me to push myself back up into a sitting position. The tears were rolling down my face as I put my clothes and shoes on, which in itself was a miracle. I did get to work on time, though every step was excruciatingly painful. Remember, I was only twenty-one at the time, but I knew what faith was and what it wasn't. I knew that I was healed no matter how it looked, that by the stripes of Jesus Christ I was healed.

When I got to work I did not tell my boss that I had been seriously hurt the day before. I walked into the office trying to keep the pain off of my face. For some reason he did not ask me what time I made it back to work. I did not tell him to change the time clock for me in order to be paid for all of the hours I was out on the job. They had me checked out at the normal quitting time. (The love of money is what causes a lot of people not to get healed.) My boss gave me an order for feed that needed to be delivered to a local farmer. If you have ever been to a feed and grain mill, you know that there is a large shoot where the feed comes out. After it has been mixed, you have to take your feed bag, and hold it up until it's filled. It creates tremendous strain on your arms and your back, even if you're healthy.

As I was filling the bag, it almost felt like I was going to pass out, because I was in tremendous pain. Now, I'm simply saying, "In the name of Jesus, in the name of Jesus, in the name of Jesus" under my breath. The second bag was even more difficult than the first bag, but I kept on saying, "In the name of Jesus." I began on the third bag and as I was speaking the name of Jesus, the power of God hit my back and I was instantly and completely, totally healed from the top of my head, to the tip of my toes. I was healed as I went on my way. My place of employment never did know what had happened to me. That has been 38 years ago, and my back is still healed by the stripes of Christ to this day.

CHAPTER TWO
#6 My Wife's Heart Murmur Healed (1978)

I was standing outside The Mount Union Christian Center, on a ladder one day, putting up new letters on the marquee, when I heard behind me the sweetest voice I had ever heard. The voice said, "Praise the Lord, Brother!" I turned around on the ladder. And there before me I saw a beautiful, blue-eyed blonde. I said back in return, "Praise God, Sister!" Immediately the Spirit of God spoke to my heart and said: ***she is your wife!*** All I could think at the moment was, *wow!* To be honest, I was quite overwhelmed.

This blue-eyed girl and I spoke for a little while. She told me that her name was Kathleen, and that she was home taking a break from college. She was one of the lead vocalists for a Christian college in Phoenixville, Pennsylvania. Actually, she was not even really supposed to be home, but God had arranged it. I did not tell her what the Spirit of God had said to me, until after we were married.

Proverbs 29:11 says, "A fool uttereth all of his mind, but a wise man keeps it in till afterwards."

When Kathleen walked away, I got down from the ladder and I went into the old movie theater. I was so filled with the spirit of joy that I jumped up upon the back of the old, unstable, theater chairs. I ran on the back of these chairs all the way down to the front of the theater, spun around, and ran back to the rear of the theater on top of the chairs again. As I was running, I was shouting, "She's the one! She's the one!" Five months later we were gloriously married.

Now here we were enjoying our time together on our honeymoon. One night I simply laid my head on my wife's chest, enjoying her closeness. I could hear her heart beating away, but to my shock and dismay the rhythm of her heart was all wrong. It sounded more clunky and noisy then what I ever imagined a heart could sound. It would beat a couple times, skip, clank, and start it all over again. Immediately fear hit my heart, and I heard the devil say to me: yeah God gave you this beautiful bride, but she will be dead in a couple years.

I said to my wonderful bride: Baby Doll what is going on with your heart? She said what? I said: your heart is not beating right. I explained to her the sound I was hearing. She informed me: yes, I was born with a heart murmur, and there is nothing the doctors can do about it.

The sound that my wife's heart was making was not just the sound of blood flowing through her valves, but it was a clicking, a clacking terrible sound. The devil was telling me that she was going to die an early death, but I was not going to have anything to do with it. **Faith** rose up in my heart at that moment. I told my wife: In the **Name of Jesus**, it has got to go. Your heart will be normal, I told her, In the **Name of Jesus**! I laid my hands upon her chest and took authority over the affliction, commanding it to go. I commanded her heart to be normal In the **Name of Jesus**! I spoke life over her, declaring she would live and not die.

After I prayed for her, I encouraged her, along with me to begin to praise God **she was healed**. Together we both lifted our hands towards heaven thanking God that **she was healed** of this heart affliction. From that moment forward we began to praise God that this heart murmur was gone. I waited for approximately 2 to 3 months before I put my head back to her chest in order to listen to her heartbeat. All of her life she was afflicted with this heart murmur, but I declared it could not stay, and that she was healed.

Approximately 2 to 3 months later as we laid in bed, once again I put my head to her chest, listening to her heartbeat. **Praise God her heart was beating normal. Thank You Jesus**! From that time(1978) to now,(2016) her heart is beating strong, healthy, and normal. God still heals, and does miracles.

"GOD Healed Me HE Will Heal YOU"

#7 Lady Miraculously Healed at Giants! 6/23/2017-- 5:35 PM

    The Bible tells us to be ready in season and out of season. My wife wanted me to go shopping with her at Giants in Gettysburg Pennsylvania. Believe me, I do not like to go shopping. But I simply agreed to go with her to pick up supplies for a work party we have going on tomorrow at the church.

    We arrived at Giants and began to go up and down the aisles shopping. Because it is a Friday, it was extremely busy. After we had filled up the cart, we ended up front in line at one of the counters. There were two people who were in front of us. The teller who is running the scanner, and collecting money was going through a very bad time. She probably was a lady in her late 50s. She just kept on hacking.

    It hurt just to hear her because it was not just a deep painful cough, but more like a hack. It kind of reminded me someone who has tuberculosis. She was trying to catch her breath, and at the same time, she was hacking. Her face was turning red the whole time that I was in line to get my groceries.

    When I finally stood before her, with her hacking, I asked her if she had water. She breathed out a yes, in between her hacking, and her trying to breathe. Now, my wife was right in front of me getting ready to bake the groceries. At that moment the compassion of God rose up in my heart.

    I told this lady: That's Enough! I said to her: let's get rid of this problem. I said to her: give me your hand. I know this was the divine authority of Christ speaking through me. Immediately she stretched forth her left hand, and I took her hand with my left hand. I then told her: put your other hand on your chest! Immediately she took her right hand, and put it upon her chest.

As I was giving her these directions, people were standing there watching it all happen. After she had her hand on her chest, I had put my right hand over her hand. I said: In the Name of Jesus Christ I command this cough to go. I said: **in the name of Jesus You Spirit of Infirmity Come Out of Her Now!**

The minute I got done praying I took my hand off her hand from her chest. And let go of her hand that I was holding. I informed her that it was done. Immediately the deep hacking cough she had been experiencing, was completely Gone. From that moment forward until we had paid the bill, loaded the groceries, and walked away from her, she did not experience one more cough.

If we would just have the boldness, and be led by the compassion of Christ we can still see miracles wherever we go. There Is Power, Authority, And Life in the **Name of Jesus Christ of Nazareth!**

Galatians 3:13 Christ hath redeemed us from the curse of the law, being made a curse for us: for it is written, Cursed is every one that hangeth on a tree:

#8 Precious Lady Delivered from Seizures (1980)

My wife and I had completed Bible college, moving back to Pennsylvania to pastor a small church. Basically, God had put it upon my heart to pay off the debt of this church (independent), and to close it down for that it would not leave a bad witness in the community. Once this was completed we began to attend different churches as the spirit of God let us. On one Sunday morning my wife and I attended an Assembly of God church in Three Springs, Pennsylvania. As the pastor was preaching there was a commotion about six pews in front of us.

"GOD Healed Me HE Will Heal YOU"

A woman who was probably in her late 30s had gone into a terrible epileptic seizure. She had fallen off her pew, and was now laying in the aisle between the pews kicking and flailing about. What was so strange is that everybody in the church ignored her, And the Pastor Kept Preaching like everything was normal. My wife and I looked at each other wondering what was going on. I asked the lady next to us in a whisper what was happening? She whispered back, informing us that this lady had seizures all the time, and there was nothing they could do. Everybody had simply learned just to act like nothing was wrong.

I could not believe what I was hearing. There was no way that I was going to sit here watching this woman tormented by the devil while this pastor continued to preach. I whispered to my wife, telling her I would be right back. I got up out of my pew, walking up to the pew where she was still having this seizure on the floor. I walked over to where she was having her seizure, and bending down to put my hands on her squirming body. I whispered: you Foul spirit in the name of Jesus Christ loose her Right Now!

Then I removed my hands waiting for the manifestation of my command to be fulfilled. Within less than one minute she stopped squirming, her eyes refocused, and she was okay. I helped her get up to sit down. Her mouth and her face were covered with spit and saliva. I could tell that this lady was not altogether there mentally. When I was done helping her, I went back to my pew.

During this whole time, the congregation just went on with the service, and the pastor just kept preaching. Even though this woman desperately needed help, they had not helped her. Why? I believe it is because they did not understand the authority that we have in Jesus Christ, when we are submitted to God. Now this is not the end of this story. It was not very long after that this pastor of this church moved on to another church, and they were looking for a new pastor. My wife's grandmother was a member of this church, and she informed me that they were looking for a new pastor. I told her that because I was not an Assembly of God minister they would not be able to hire me. During me explaining this to Kathee's grandmother, the Lord spoke to my heart, telling me I would be the next pastor.

Arrangements were made, and I sat down with the church board letting them know that I would be glad to fill-in, and preach for them until they found another pastor. (I did not tell them that God had spoken to my heart, informing me that I would be there next pastor. That was God's job, not mine.) They had me come and minister, and God moved mightily in every one of these services. The next thing I knew, they were asking me to be their pastor. They said because I was not an Assembly of God minister, I would have to go before those who oversaw our district. I agreed to do this. The man who was over the Pennsylvania district was in Camp Hill Pennsylvania. His name was Philip Buongiorno who was the superintendent of the Pennsylvania, and Delaware District of the Assemblies of God.

I arrived on the prearranged date to speak with the superintendent. He was an elderly man, who I could tell had a deep relationship with God. He began to ask me questions about my life, experiences, and education. When I was done speaking, and answering his questions, he simply looked at me and said: I Never Interfere with What God Is Doing! He then shook my hand, informing me that I was the new pastor of Three Springs Assembly of God Church.

Now back to my story about Norma: as long as I was pastor at Three Springs, I never allowed the devil to manifest himself in my services again by Norma having a seizure. Before the service I would pray with her taking authority over these demonic spirits afflicting her. I also told her that we could help her in getting free. My wife and I sat down with her one day asking her when these seizures began. She informed us that when she was a little girl she had a terrible accident and had damaged her head. Because of this accident they had taken her to the hospital where the doctors had to perform an operation. They told her parents that there was water buildup on her brain. They had literally drilled down into her skull to get to this buildup to release the pressure.

"GOD Healed Me HE Will Heal YOU"

The operation did succeed in this regard, but with two bad results. First: from that moment forward she was never the same mentally. Her mind had never completely fully developed. She was slow in speech, and slow in her actions. She was no simpleton, but her mind simply never developed. The second problem was: that she had terrible seizures all the time. No matter what medication they gave her, it did not seem to be able to stop these seizures.

I told her I would pray about her situation. I'm sorry to say that I had ministers come through our church who prayed for Norma prophesying that she would never have another seizure after they prayed for her. There prophecies proved false, because these seizures continued. As I sought the Lord about this situation for Norma he informed me that Norma was not demon possessed, (which I knew) but that these demonic powers would come upon her at different times to oppressor her. The Lord gave me specific instructions on how to help Norma overcome these seizures. We sat her down again, asking her if she could tell when the seizures were going to happen.

In the beginning she said that she could not tell, and that there were no warning signs. We went a little bit deeper with questioning. I asked her if there was at any time she seemed to be getting confused, upset, disorientated, or aggravated. She sat there for a while thinking about my question. She said: Yes, now that you have asked me this question, I do seem to get confused, or aggravated, disorientated right before I have a seizure.

I told her: okay Norma, this is what I want you to do. The next time these emotions, feelings begin to come upon you, I want you to stop everything at once. Take the name of Jesus and say: In the Name of Jesus Christ I command you devil go from me now, In Jesus Name! I said Norma keep saying: In Jesus Name, in Jesus name That, In Jesus Name! Keep saying it to yourself until all the feelings of confusion, aggravation, disorientation, or anger leaves. She agreed that she would do this. Now, through the week I would usually get phone calls from her family asking us to pray because she had a terrible seizure. All that week we did not hear another word about her.

When she came to the church the next Sunday she was filled with great joy. She informed us that she had not had any seizures because she had followed my directions. She had a week free from seizures which was so amazing, and wonderful for her.
There were times she still had seizures after this, but she informed us it was whenever she did not use the name of Jesus quick enough when she was being hit with these feelings of confusion, frustration, disorientation, or anger.

After this she ran into another challenge. Instead of having seizures during the day, she began to have very terrible seizures in her sleep. She was devastated by the fact that she was not yet free. I told her by the spirit of God that if she would take authority over these demonic powers before she went to sleep, that these seizures would not happen to her. She agreed to take the name of Jesus, binding the enemy before she went to bed. To her great delight when she remembered to use her authority over the enemy In the Name of Jesus as she went to bed, the seizures never happened. The last time we seen Norma, (I left that church to be a missionary to Europe,) she was still free of these seizures. **Whom the Son Sets Free, Is Free Indeed!**

#9 Raising The Dead At Cracker Barrel! (2016)

One morning in the middle of November of 2016, my wife asked me to take her to breakfast at Cracker Barrel. "Normally we only eat at Cracker Barrel when Joanna and Randy Herndon (Joanna is the daughter of the late great Jack Coe) are staying at our church." I agreed to her request, informing her that I would love to go eat breakfast with her at Cracker Barrel. From where we pastor in Gettysburg, PA, it is about a 20-minute drive.

"GOD Healed Me HE Will Heal YOU"

We arrived at Cracker Barrel around 10 AM. One of the waitresses took us to our table which was in about the middle of the restaurant. We were sitting and simply discussing the how good and wonderful God has been to us. We ordered our breakfast meal. Eventually, the food arrived, and we held hands thanking God for our food, and for his divine guidance in our lives. We ate our food leisurely enjoying each other's company. When out of the blue two waitresses began to walk briskly down the length of the restaurant urgently asking if there was any doctor or nurse available. The way they were calling out you could tell that something urgent and tragic was going on.

In most of these similar situations, I would be immediately upon my feet heading to the problem area. One time I was at (in about 1996) Lowe's with my family shopping when a similar situation happened. One of the tellers had gone into an epileptic seizure. I immediately ran over to the counter informing them that I was a doctor (Ph.D. in biblical theology) and that I could help. In that situation, I simply leaned over the counter and laid my hands on the girl who was having a seizure and was thrashing about. I took authority very quietly commanding the devil to let her go. Immediately the seizure stopped, and she jumped up to her feet.

Now here I was in a seemingly similar situation. What is so strange though is that I did not sense any urgency in my heart to go help at that moment. It did not occur to me until after this event that for some reason I had not acted in my regular routine method. Now that I look back, I believe that God was in this. My wife and I simply sat there, talking back and forth a little bit, and finishing our meal.

Approximately 10 minutes later we simply got to our feet and began to walk towards the front of the restaurant. As we got to the opening of the entrance to the restaurant we noticed a small crowd had gathered. As we walked up to this crowd I could see that there is a woman who was leaning over the top of a rather large lady who was laying on her left side, on the floor with her body completely extended. This lady who was laying out on the floor was completely still. There was no movement from her whatsoever. There was a very heavy blanket of silence over the whole crowd, with nobody talking. Everybody's eyes were upon the lady who was laying on the hardwood floor completely still.

When I saw this lady laid out upon the floor the compassion of God rose up in my heart, and immediately overwhelmed me. When the love of God begins the flood when your heart to this extent, the best thing to do is simply to surrender to the divine impulse at work inside of you. In my heart, it was as if the lady laying on the floor was a very personal person to me. I had to do something and at that very moment, I was motivated to get involved. I walked over to the crowd and very gently pushed my way through. I spoke up informing them that I was a local pastor and that I would like to help. I did not have to push my way through, they simply made room for me to come through.

The woman who was bending over this lady on the floor informed me that she was a nurse. She had a hold of one of the hands of the lady on the floor. I could see that she had her fingers on her wrist, looking for a heartbeat. I knelt down next to her. This lady who was laying on the floor looked to be in her mid to late-60s. She was laying on her left side completely still. Tears began to fill my eyes, and I reached forth my hand and place it upon her cheek. I discovered that her cheek was extremely cold to my touch.

I have learned in over 40 years of moving in the spirit that you do not have to pray aloud prayer or shout at the enemy. (Them that do know their God shall be strong and do exploits) With the love of God flowing in my heart, I prayed a very simple prayer in Jesus name. I commanded the spirit of infirmity to go and began speaking life over her very quietly in Jesus name. As I'm praying for this lady, tears were filling my eyes. I felt as if I knew her personally and that she was someone who was important to me. This is how the Holy Spirit works. God has shed His love abroad in our hearts by the Holy Ghost. It is in this realm that the gift of faith will begin to operate. You're not leaning on the understanding of your mind, or operating in simple human sympathy.

"GOD Healed Me HE Will Heal YOU"

In probably less than a minute as I was praying the nurse spoke up very excitedly and made this statement: She Has a Pulse! As I thought about this later it became obvious to me that this lady up to that moment had lost her pulse. I continue to pray softly, as I still had my right hand on her cheek very softly. The next thing I knew this lady who was laying on the floor began to stir, and she reached up her right hand and put it on my hand squeezing it.

I knew in my heart that my job was done. The spirit of Christ had touched this precious lady, raising her from the dead. There were no fireworks, explosions, or loud shouting, but simply the gentle moving of the Spirit of Christ. The resurrection power of God manifested without people even realizing it.

I got up from my kneeling position, walking back to the crowd. My wife was simply waiting for me to complete the task. As we walked out the door of Cracker Barrel, the ambulance was coming around the corner, with its lights flashing. We simply walked out to our car and got into it. We took a minute to thank God once again for confirmed the authority and power that we have in the Name of Jesus, with signs following.

CHAPTER THREE

#10 When I Was Brought Back to Life (1980)

I woke up one morning extremely sick. My whole body ached from my head to my toes, even to the ends of my fingers. It felt as if I had been pulled through a knothole. I cried out to God and came against this satanic sickness. However, I grew worse, and worse all day long. I had an extremely high fever with sweat just pouring off of my body.

Kathee would pray for me throughout the day. I knew I had to shake this thing, whatever it was. So I went outside and began to climb the mountain behind our house. Every thirty feet or so I would get so dizzy that I had to stop and put my hands on my knees with my head bowed to the ground. When this happened I would pray hard. Dizziness and fatigue kept hitting me like the waves of the ocean. After a while I would begin to climb the mountain side again, and it wasn't long before I'd have to stop and bend over again. It felt like I would pass out any second, but I kept on declaring that I would live, and not die.

I think this is where many people make a major mistake: their faith is a passive faith; but biblical, God-given faith is not passive, but it is aggressive and violent. I finally made it up to the top of this small mountain. I remembered where there was a log lying on the ground, so I sat down next to it, and fell unto my back. I just laid there and prayed. When I say I prayed, I mean I kept praising God, thanking God that by the stripes of Jesus Christ I was healed. Eventually, I pushed myself back up, and began to go back down the mountain. When I finally saw the parsonage, I was filled with great relief. I went into the house, feeling worse than ever. I asked Kathee to pray with me. She stayed and prayed at my side. I was burning up with a fever and I needed to get my clothes off. I went to our little bathroom and stripped down to nothing. I was going through terrible flashes. I lay on the linoleum floor hoping to absorb some of its coolness.

Then something frightening happened. I began to sense in a real way that I was going to die. It wasn't exactly fear; it was just something I knew. I cried out to Kathee to come to me. She came into the bathroom and sat down on the floor, putting my head on her lap, praying fervently for me. I could feel my life slowly ebbing out. The next thing I knew my spirit and soul were leaving my body. I was above my wife, looking down upon my body, with my head in her lap. She was crying out to God for me. For a while I simply hovered over the top of myself and my wife. There was no pain or sickness racking me anymore. There was just a total complete peace.

My wife must have noticed that I had died, and she began to commanding me to **LIVE in Jesus Name**! Suddenly, as she was commanding, I felt myself being pulled back rapidly into my body. It was like somebody had turned on a vacuum cleaner and sucked me back into my body. I came to my senses with my head in her lap. It felt like a cold wind was now blowing over my whole body me. I was totally, completely, and instantly healed! The fever and sickness was completely gone. If you ask my opinion of what happened on that day, I literally believe that I died, but my wife's prayers, and her taking authority in Jesus Name brought me back.

#11 Cancer Patient Raised from the Bed of Death

One morning I received a phone call from my good friend, Paul. He told me that he knew of a man who owned a logging company and lumber yard who was about to die. They were waiting for him to expire any day because his body was filled with cancer. Most of it was concentrated in his chest and it had spread throughout the rest of his body. He was located in the McConnellsburg hospital. Paul asked me if I would be willing to go pray for him. I asked him to give me one day to fast and pray for this particular situation. I spent the rest of that day in prayer, fasting, and in the Word.

The next morning Paul came to pick me up. We drove up to the McConnellsburg hospital, praying as we went. We walked into the foyer and up to the information desk. The nurse gave us the necessary information we needed. Paul said he would wait for me and that he would continue in prayer in the hospital's chapel. I found the room where they had put this gentleman, knocked on the door, and entered. They had placed him in a very small room—just big enough to be a closet—that was off the beaten path, like they were just waiting for him to die. He was lying on a hospital bed and was nothing but skin and bones; he looked as if he had just come out of a concentration camp. His skin and the whites of his eyes were yellow. He was a rather tall man who looked to be in his late sixties. He was lying on his bed wide awake. I had no idea what his mental condition was. I began to speak to him and discovered he was totally aware of his surroundings, and actually, I was amazed at how clear and quick his mind was.

I began to speak to him by introducing myself. He almost seemed to take an antagonistic attitude towards me right away. I began to share Jesus with him, but as I was speaking to him, a smirk appeared on his face. He began to tell me stories of the things he had seen in church— supernatural things. He said one time he was in a wild church service where everybody was jumping and shouting. It was quite a number of years ago, and they did not yet have electricity in this church. He said as he was watching people dance and shout, one of them jumped so high that he hit a lighted kerosene lantern, causing it to fall off of the hook. It came crashing down onto the floor and should have immediately broken into pieces and caught the building on fire. Instead, he said it almost acted like a ball. It never broke or went out but landed straight up. The people just kept on dancing and singing to the Lord.

After he told me this story he looked me right in the eyes and said to me, "If I did not get saved back then, what makes you think

"GOD Healed Me HE Will Heal YOU"

you are going to get me saved now?" I did not answer him. My heart was filled with deep sorrow and overwhelming love for him. I knew I could not help him, and if was going to get saved and be healed it was going to take God moving upon him supernaturally. I stepped away from his deathbed, and I bowed my head and cried out to God. "Lord, touch this man, help me to reach him because I cannot do it within myself. Lord, You're going to have to touch his heart or he will lose his soul and end up in hell." As I was praying under my breath I sensed the awesome presence of God come flooding into that little hospital room.

Then the Spirit of the Lord rose up within me, and I walked back over to his bed. I began to speak to Elvin once again, but it was under a divine unction of great compassion. I know I did not say very much, but as I was speaking, all of a sudden out of the blue, he began to weep uncontrollably. In just a matter of seconds his heart was completely open to the gospel. He gave his heart to Jesus Christ right then and there. Then I laid my hands on him and commanded his body to be healed. I rebuked the spirit of death, and cancer in the name of Jesus Christ, commanding it to go.

When I was done praying, it seemed to me there was some immediate improvement in his countenance and body. I told him as I got ready to leave that I would visit him again in the hospital. After I left something wonderful happened, but I did not hear the story until later that day when I arrived home from the hospital. Immediately Elvin felt healed in his body. His appetite came back, and the yellow jaundice disappeared completely from his skin and from the white of his eyes. The hospital personnel were amazed at this transformation. They took some new x-rays and discovered that the cancer he had in his body was almost totally gone. The cancer that was in his lungs which had been the size of a baseball was now the size of a cashew nut. In three days' time they released him from the hospital and sent him home. He was working at his sawmill with his son and grandsons within a week!

#12 Unbelieving Man Healed (1980)

One day as I was preaching in the tent, a man who looked to be in his mid-thirties was hobbling by really slow on a pair of crutches. He was not even looking in the direction of our tent, but was looking straight ahead, minding his own business. As I looked at him, the Spirit of God quickened the gift of faith inside of me. When God quickens my heart in this way I do not even think what I'm about to do. I simply act upon the quickening and the witness in my heart. I found myself calling out to this particular man, speaking over the microphone system. Everybody could hear me within a hundred feet, if not further. Probably the whole Huntington Fair could hear us! (Actually the fire department was really upset with us because we were disturbing their bingo games.) I called out to this man but he ignored me. Once again I challenged him to come into the tent so God could heal him. This time he looked my way but kept hobbling along. I called out the third time, encouraging him to come and be healed of his problem.

After the third time, he finally came into the tent. When he came to the front, I asked him if he had faith to believe that God would heal him. He looked at me as if I had lost my mind. He was probably thinking, *You're the one who called me up here. I don't even know what this is about. Everybody was staring at me, so I had to come!* He did not respond to my question. I told him that I was going to pray for him now and God would heal him! I asked him again if he believed this. Once again he did not respond. Then I laid my hands on him and commanded his leg to be healed In the name of Jesus Christ of Nazareth.

After I was done praying, I told him to put down his crutches and start walking without them. He stood there staring at me. Everybody else was also staring at me. This was okay because the gift of faith was at work in my heart. I reached forward and took away his crutches. I threw them on the ground and spun him around. When I'm in this realm I'm not thinking, I'm simply acting. Then I pushed him, and he stumbled forward and began to walk toward the back of the tent. He was picking his legs high up in the air, high stepping it. When he got to the edge of the tent he spun back toward me. Tears were streaming from his eyes and down his cheeks. He came back toward me walking perfectly normal with no limp whatsoever!

I gave him the microphone, and asked him to tell us what did God do for him. He kept saying, "You don't understand" over and over. Once again, I encouraged him to tell us his story. I had him face the people in that tent and those outside of the tent who had been watching. He told us that last winter he had been walking on a very icy sidewalk and he lost his footing. Slipping and sliding, he fell forward onto the concrete and ice. He fell down so hard on his kneecap that he had done something terrible to it. He could not move his knee whatsoever, and it was extremely painful. He went to the doctor's office and they x-rayed it. The x-rays revealed that his kneecap had literally been shattered and destroyed. In just two more days he was scheduled to have a major operation to replace his kneecap.

I encouraged him to go back to his doctor and get it x-rayed again, and to come back and tells us the doctors report. Sure enough, a couple days later he came back to the tent giving a wonderful testimony. He had gone to his doctor. He said when he walked into the doctor's office they could tell that his knee was normal. The doctor asked him what had happened. He told them about the encounter he had with Jesus at our tent meeting. They x-rayed his kneecap and discovered he had a brand-new kneecap!

#13 Victory over Tumors (1981)

I woke up one morning with tremendous pain in my lower abdomen. I lifted up my shirt and looked down where the pain was. There was a lump on my abdomen about the size of an acorn. I laid my hands on it immediately, commanding it to go.

I said "You lying devil, by the stripes of Jesus I am healed and made whole." After I spoke to the lump, the pain became excruciating and overwhelmingly worse. All that day I walked the floor crying out to God, and praising him that His Word is real and true. I went for a walk on the mountain right behind the parsonage.

It was a long day before I got to sleep that night. When I awoke the next morning the pain was even more severe. It felt like somebody was stabbing me in my gut with a knife. I lifted up my shirt and looked and there was another lump. Now I had two lumps in my lower abdomen.

I laid my hands on them, commanding them to go. Tears were rolling down my face, as I spoke the Word. I lifted my hands toward heaven and kept praising God that I was healed. Even though I did not see any change, I kept praising God. All the symptoms were telling me that God's Word is a lie, and that I was not healed by the stripes of Jesus. But I knew that I was healed. It was another long day. It seemed as if I could never get to sleep that night. The pain was continual and non-stop!

When I got up the next morning the pain had intensified even more. Once again I looked at my abdomen and to my shock there was another lump the size of an acorn. Now I had three of these nasty lumps and each were about the size of an acorn. I did not think that the pain could get any worse, but it was. Once again I laid my hands on these tumors, commanding them to go in the name of Jesus Christ of Nazareth. I declared that by the stripes of

Jesus I am healed! It felt like a knife sticking in my gut all that day and night. I lifted my hands, and with tears rolling down my face, kept praising God that I was healed. By faith I began to dance before the Lord a victory dance, praising God that I was healed by the stripes of Jesus. I went to bed that night hurting worse than ever. All night I tossed and turned and moaned, all the while thanking God that I was not going to die but that I was healed. I got up the next morning, and all of the tumors and pain were gone. They have never come back.

#14 How I Take My Healing - May 5, 2017

"GOD Healed Me HE Will Heal YOU"

What I'm about to tell you will sound extremely strange if you do not understand how faith talks, walks and reacts to the circumstances of life. You cannot fake faith, or just confess it into existence. Faith is when you know, that you know, that you know, that you know God's word is true, and he cannot lie. It is when what God has said is more real to you than what your bodies telling you, circumstances, symptoms, or the experts of this world.

This morning, May 5, 2017, my sons and daughter law went with me to get a load of firewood someone gave us. In the process of loading approximately a cord and 1/2 of firewood, my right foot began to hurt real bad. That's the same foot that I slammed down in about 1996 when it was broke. The fifth time I slammed my foot down, (1996) it was instantly healed. I did this underneath and unction of the gift of faith.

Today we were loading this firewood, and my foot began to really hurt. I did not say a word to my sons or my daughter-in-law. I just continue to work, under my breath telling the devil that he was a liar, and telling my foot that it was healed. The symptoms did not dissipate or leave me in the least. After we loaded the firewood, we went and ate at a Chinese restaurant, we got home. Now the boys got busy unloading this firewood. I walked across the parking lot of our church to my office which is approximately 400 feet away. My foot was hurting so bad by this time, that it was hard to put any weight on it whatsoever.

I got into my office and began to do some office work. I needed to go all the way to the front of our facility to get a room ready for a guest speaker. This room is approximately 150 feet away from where my office is. As I went my foot seemed to be getting worse. Of course, the devil he's yakking away at me, but I'm simply ignoring him.

I get done with the preparation and I walked out of the room I was preparing, and OH man was my foot hurting. The spirit of faith rose up in me at that moment, and I slammed my right foot down real hard. I Said, Devil, you're a Liar, and my foot is healed. I took about 20 more steps and it was getting worse. Once again, I said: Devil You're a Liar, and my foot is healed. I slammed my right foot down again real hard. I took about another 10 steps, and the devil was telling me that I have got a major problem and that I won't be able to get rid of this foot problem so quick and easy.

In my heart I laughed at the devil because I have been through so much worse than this. The third time I slammed my foot down, speaking to the devil and my foot. Devil in the Name of Jesus You're a Liar, and my foot is healed. I went on my way rejoicing and ignoring the pain. I did not try to step lightly, but I made myself walk normally.

By the time I went the hundred feet or more to my office, the pain was completely gone, and I was healed. Let me say that the manifestation of my healing was evident in my foot. I am not bragging about Mike Yeager, I am breaking about Jesus Christ, and the word of God. God cannot lie! Pastor Mike what if the manifestation would not have happened so soon? My answer to that is: SO, WHAT!

Yes, I mean: So What! Let God be true, and everything else a lie. If you are not walking in this area, this realm, simply begin to give yourself to the word of God, in prayer and meditation until it explodes in your heart. Unto the Reality of the Truth overwhelms the lie.

The Lord spoke to my heart one Sunday morning as I was in prayer getting ready for church. He said this to me: Is the darkness greater than the light? I said: No Lord! The Lord said to me: The Darkness Has No Power over the Light! The minute you step into the light the darkness must flee! It Has No Choice! This is how the kingdom of God works! Whatever is born of God, overcomes the world by faith in Christ. All I can say is: Thank You, Jesus! Oh, if only we would submit completely to King Jesus! Oh, if only we would submit to his Lordship in every area! What miracles we would see wherever we go!

CHAPTER FOUR

#15 Arthritis Could Not Stay! (1996 up to now)

There are generational curses that are passed on from one generation to another. These are satanic strongholds that must be broken. In my family lineage, there were quite a number of these strongholds. My personal family members and I have, and had numerous physical infirmities.

When I gave my heart to Jesus Christ and began to intensely study the word of God, I discovered that I was free from the curse of the law. I began to aggressively take what Christ had purchased for me with the stripes on His back. By faith, I began to cast down these physical strongholds. Not only did I receive healing for my own personal body, but I also declared that in the name of Jesus these physical afflictions would not be passed on any longer. My sons and daughters and their children would not have these afflictions.

One of these afflictions that were passed on from generation to generation is arthritis. My sister Deborah began to experience arthritis in her late 20s. At one time she had been a very gifted typist and piano player, but before she was in her 40s, her fingers had become gnarled and almost unusable. Arthritis had entered her body so dramatically that I remember her crying with pain and great suffering.

By my late 20s and early 30s arthritis began to try to manifest itself in the joints of my fingers. The minute that pain came to my hands I began to boldly speak to them even as Jesus declared in the Gospel of Mark 11:23.

Mark 11:23 For verily I say unto you, that whosoever shall say unto this mountain, ***Be thou removed, and be thou cast into the sea; and shall not doubt in his heart, but shall believe that those things which he saith shall come to pass; he shall have whatsoever he saith.***

I submitted myself to God, resisted the devil by speaking to the affliction and commanding it to go. And then I began to praise God, and thank God that by faith I was healed In the Name of Jesus. No matter how my hands or fingers felt I thank God that I was healed.

Sure enough, after a day or two, the stiffening and pain would completely dissipate from my joints. Through the years it has tried to come back over and over, but I have not allowed it. I know this may sound braggadocios, but it's not. This is a reality that Christ has given to every believer!

And being not weak in faith, he considered not his own body now dead, when he was about an hundred years old, neither yet the deadness of Sara's womb: He staggered not at the promise of God through unbelief; but was strong in faith, giving glory to God; And being fully persuaded that, what he had promised, he was able also to perform (Romans 4:19-21).

#16 Healed Me of 3 Major Problems! (1985)

Darlene writes: My healing occurred either late in the year of 1985 or early in the year of 1986. For 8 months I had an anorexia eating disorder which then led to anemia which led to loss of the monthly cycle and no longer ovulating (barren), as well as not being able to have bowel movements. Now remember I said the situation was like that for 8 months. I had constipation and no matter what I used, it seldom helped. I just wasn't eating enough. I had what looked like bruising from the top of my spine to the bottom of it. That is what my back looked like. I was around 16 or 17 years old at the time and only weighed 86 lbs.

When my dad realized how thin I was getting and the symptoms and illnesses that were happening in my body, he decided to go on a fast while he worked as a welder full time. All he had during the fast was juice and water.

During the fast, my family and I went to the garage old building in Cash town where you held church services. We were going there on a regular basis. You called out 3 of the issues that I needed healed of. I walked up front, believing to receive my healing. You prayed for me and within a week's time each issue one at a time was healed. The doctor when he took another test to check for anaemia and found that there was no longer an issue anymore, couldn't believe it. I started gaining weight like crazy.

God's wondrous works are amazing. Now me and my sons pray for people and people sometimes fall down under the power and get healed in different areas. Words of wisdom! I remember when I was in my early 20's the power of God would also come down through my arms and I would pray for people and they would be healed. Some were in the hospital with heart problems.

#17 Charity Raised from the Bed of Death (1985)

Back in 1985 we had a wonderful couple that were very active in our church. This brother actually went to the Philippines with me on a number of occasions. His profession was that he hung and finished drywall, in which he was extremely gifted and he worked very fast. Actually he has done quite a number of jobs for the church, including doing all our drywall when we put up our new facility. One day while he was gone to work his daughter Charity became congested, and was having difficulty breathing. His wife not knowing what to do because it seemed like it was pretty bad, ran her into the emergency room. Now that is when their nightmare began. They immediately wanted to admit her to the hospital. Well instead of her getting better, she got worse. The parents wanted to take her home and see what they could do, but the hospital would not allow them. The hospital basically decided to ship her off to Hershey Medical Centre.

My wife and I made an emergency trip down to see her, because she was getting worse. Charity at this time I think was probably less than 10 years old. When I walked into her hospital room, personally I became extremely upset. Here they had her hospital bed directly underneath an air conditioning vent. The cold air was being pumped down on top of her, with her wearing a very thin nightgown. Not only was she wearing a very thin nightgown, but because of the fact that she wanted to go home with her parents, they had strapped her to the bed, like she was some kind of criminal.

I have had dealings with the medical world even before I was born again. After I was born again, a part of my PhD training was through a local hospital, in which they had an accredited program. I know a lot of people think highly of the medical world, but I am sorry to say I have seen too much on the other side.

One of the head nurses for a local Hospital back in the early 80s, was the wife of one of my elders. She would tell me stories that were unbelievable of the things that she saw the doctors do. She literally was tormented even though she was the head nurse for surgery. My youth pastor's wife's brother-in-law was a doctor, and she could not believe the things that he would say about his patients, and the amount of money he was hauling in.

In sharing this story, I am not at all trying to create animosity towards them. I realize there are a lot of sincere people in the medical profession. I also realize that there are a lot of people who would be dead without medical help. On the other side of the

"GOD Healed Me HE Will Heal YOU"

equation I personally know a lot of people who would still be alive, if they would not have believed everything they were told by the medical world.

So here poor little Charity is strapped to the bed with a very thin nightgown, the air conditioning is being pumped over the top of her, and she is shivering and getting worse every moment. It upset me so much, that I did mention something to one of the medical personnel, but they simply ignored me. We prayed for her, with a heavy heart, knowing that if God did not intervene, they would literally kill her. There is nobody who could be strapped to a bed on their back, with cold air-conditioning being dumped on them 24 hours a day and not end up with pneumonia. This is exactly what happened to Charity, but not just pneumonia, but double pneumonia. Both of her lungs were now filled with pneumonia and fluid.

We kept in constant contact with the parents about their little girl. The hospital was now calling every shot when it came to what they were going to do with her. They actually ended cutting open both of her lungs, to scrape out the congestion, and the parts of the lungs that had died.

Right after this operation, the father came into my office. They had been saving up money in order to build a house. He informed me that he had heard from heaven, and that he was taking a step of faith by giving to the church all the money they had saved up for building a new house. He said he needed a miracle for their little girl, and this was their seed of faith. At that moment I actually tried to talk him out of giving this money, telling him that you could not buy a miracle from God. I said this to him very gently because I knew they were fighting for their daughter's life, and they were having to deal with the medical world that was literally killing their little girl before their very eyes. He told me that he and his wife had prayed, and that they had definitely heard from heaven about this financial gift that they needed to make to the church. You see we also needed a miracle, because if I did not have $50,000 in just a couple weeks I was going to jail. That's another story.

What could I do, but tell him that if he had heard from heaven, we would accept his gift. We held hands and we prayed together, believing God to divinely intervene for their little girl Charity. He left the office, believing that they had obeyed God, and that somehow God was going to divinely intervene.

Now remember they had tried over and over to try to get her out of the hands of the medical world. It is not because they did not believe in medicine or medical help, but they saw them killing their little girl. If you do not believe that the medical world kills a lot of people, you are simply ignorant, or you have chosen to ignore the facts. They had basically given to this couple a death sentence for their daughter. We all together, and especially the parents, took a hold of God for a miracle.

Three days later I received an incredible phone call from the father. He told me that his daughter was home from the hospital. In spite of everything the medical world had done to their little girl, God had instantly, and completely healed her lungs. Praise God for answered prayer, and obedience. This miracle was not bought by a financial gift, but the fact that they had literally sacrificed the down payment they needed to build their dream house. In their hearts they were saying to God, Father we do not care about that house, all we care about is our little girl. God had supernaturally heard their plea, and rescued their daughter from certain death.

It is approximately 30 years later, and their little girl has grown up and has become the mother of her own precious children. If you would ask her mom and dad was it worth the sacrifice, they would answer with a resounding yes, a million times over!

"GOD Healed Me HE Will Heal YOU"

#18 OVERCOMING SYMPTOMS OF A STROKE! 2009

Numbers 23:19 God is not a man, that he should lie; neither the son of man, that he should repent: hath he said, and shall he not do it? or hath he spoken, and shall he not make it good?

When the enemy comes in like a flood, if I will trust God, act upon the word, God will raise up a standard against the enemy. I'm amazed at how many modern believers are such pacifist when it comes to fighting off the enemy by Faith in Christ. You have to rise up in the Name of Jesus Christ and speak against the circumstance which is contrary to God's will. If the circumstance does not seem to change, you do not let go of God's promises. You maintain a thankful and worshipful heart towards the Lord. Here is an illustration in my personal life.

The other day I was lying in bed all night long with terrible pain racking my body, yet I am fighting the fight of faith, speaking the Word, and praying quietly as I'm lying in bed. I never allow a spirit of fear to control and dictate my actions.

The next thing I know my left hand went completely numb with my fingers all curled up. The devil said to me: you're having a stroke. Immediately jumped out of bed, and I took my numb left arm with its curled up fingers and began to beat it against my right hand commanding it to be healed. I knew that this circumstance was not of God because by his stripes we were healed! I had to rise in the Spirit Of Faith speaking to this circumstance in and by the Name of Jesus.

After over 40 years of practice, I know in most situations what is, and what is not the will of God. After I had commanded my arm and my hand, my body to be healed, I began to Thank the Lord that it was done. Now, in the natural, my arm and my hand were still in the same condition as it was before I spoke to it in the name of Jesus, but I know that God Cannot Lie.

Praise the Lord, within a short period of time my left arm and hand was completely restored, and all the pain left my body. This took place back in about 2009. We should never give into the lie, or the symptoms that the enemy is trying to use against us. The minute the enemy sticks his ugly head up, we need to cut it off with the word of God.

When I was a kid, we used to fish in a favorite fishing hole. It was filled with pan fish, crop-pies, and bluegills. The only problem is that it also had lots of mud turtles. These nasty turtles would kill anything that was in their path. Whenever we went fishing, we would always carry our 22 rifles. When these mud turtles stuck their heads up, we popped them with our 22 rifles.

We were not going to allow them to devour the fish we were trying to catch. If we had not done this, there would have been no fish left in this pond. It is the same way spiritually. You cannot allow the devil and his demonic host to simply run over you. We must rise up, and overcome spiritual pacifism.

Matthew 16:19 And I will give unto thee the keys of the kingdom of heaven: and whatsoever thou shalt bind on earth shall be bound in heaven: and whatsoever thou shalt loose on earth shall be loosed in heaven.

#19 Mountain Man Healed & Restored (2015)

Vicki and Linda, two sisters who attend the church I pastor, informed me that their father (in his late 70s) had suffered a terrible stroke. It was the Sunday before Thanksgiving, and they were attending our Sunday morning service. That is when I was informed that their father had a devastating and terrible stroke. The

"GOD Healed Me HE Will Heal YOU"

minute they told me, I knew in my heart that I had to get to the Chambersburg Hospital to pray for him. I told them that as soon as I could, I would get up to the hospital, even today.

It was approximately 2 PM when I arrived at the hospital. As I walked down the hospital hallway, entering the hospital elevator, and pushed the button for the third-floor, I was in deep prayer. There was great expectation in my heart that God was about to do something wonderful. When I found the hospital room, the door was hanging slightly open. I entered the room where their father was located. The room was full of family members who were obviously quite upset. On the bed laid this tall, husky, full white bearded man. He actually looks like a mountain man that you would read about in the old-time books.

The doctor was standing next to the bed and giving a report to the family. It was obvious that he was not giving them a good report. He was telling them that he could not guarantee their father would ever recover from this terrible stroke. Their father seemed to in a coma, (not that he was) for he was neither here nor there. His eyes were coated with a dull looking white color.

The Doctor told them that their father was blind, and he did not know if their father would ever recover his eyesight even if he recovered from the stroke. Everything the doctor said was negative. There were tears flowing in that hospital room that day. I just stood there quietly waiting for the doctor to finish, and then to leave. I knew that what his doctor was saying was true in the natural, but we have access to the one who created all things. I believed in my heart that day that the great physician was going to pay them a house call.

Something was stirring in my heart, and I knew what it was. It was the gift of faith that produces immediate results, causing there to be excitement and joy in believer's hearts. After the doctor walked out, I walked over to the hospital bed where William was lying in a state of what looked like death. I spoke up drawing everybody's attention to me. I told them: don't be afraid, Bill is going to be okay. I told them by the word of wisdom that his eyesight was going to come back. I told them that his mind was going to be quickened by the spirit of God, and that the Lord was going to raise him up again.

One of the family members asked me: are you sure? I said: absolutely. Now, Thanksgiving was only about four days away. I told them: I believe that he will be home for Thanksgiving! Faith rose up in all of the family members who were there. Instead of tears of sorrow, now flowed tears of great joy. Some of them began to cry out right. I said to them: now let's lay hands on William, and take care of this problem. They gathered around Williams bed, laying hands upon him. I did not pray real loud, but I prayed with authority. In the Name of Jesus, I commanded him to be healed, and we all agreed. I commanded for his eyesight, his mind, his reasoning, and his body functions to come back to normal In the Name of Jesus!

When I was done praying, with everybody in total agreement, I said: now let us praise God for Bills complete recovery. We all began to quietly praise the Lord for answered prayer. The hospital room was now filled with great joy, and peace. As I left I told them that I was expecting a good report. I encouraged them to have a wonderful Thanksgiving, and that I would be in touch with them.

About three days later I was contacted by one of the daughters of William. They were extremely excited because her father had made a complete and absolute recovery. His eyesight had come back, and his brain, mental awareness had completely returned. That Thanksgiving he was home eating turkey with the rest of the family. To the writing of this book he is still doing wonderful. Every day his children walk with him down the paths and the roads of the forest they live in, right outside of Chambersburg Pennsylvania. God still answers prayer when we pray in faith.

CHAPTER FIVE

#20 Terrible Warts Gone Over Night (1986)

A poverty-stricken couple began to come to our church. We watched as Jesus set this couple free from drugs, alcohol, violence, and immorality. We helped install a new bathroom in their little house. The wife became one of the main workers in the church. She was always there trying to help people.

One day they brought one of their young daughters to us. They told us she had a problem they did not know how to resolve. They had taken her to the doctor, but there didn't seem to be anything they could do. The girl was hiding behind them so her mother brought her to the front. Then she had the girl hold out her little hand. It was terrible. Her little hand was completely covered with warts front and back. We are not talking about twenty or thirty warts. It literally looked like hundreds of warts. We laid our hands on her little hand. We then commanded these foul warts to come off of her hand in the name of Jesus Christ of Nazareth, and for her hand to be completely healed.

As we looked at her hand, it did not seem as if anything happened. We told them that when you pray in faith, you must believe that those things you asked for in faith are done. We explained that what we need to do is begin to thank God that she is healed—that the warts are gone in the name of Jesus. Both the husband and the wife agreed that it was done. They took their little girl, got in their car, and left.

The next morning, I received a phone call from the mother. She was extremely excited and bursting with happiness. She told us that when her little girl went to bed that night nothing had changed. The warts were just as bad as ever. When she went to get her the next morning, every single wart was gone but one. They brought the little girl back to us to look at her hand. Sure enough, in one-night God had removed every single wart but one, which was in the palm of her hand! The skin on her hand was smooth and normal just like the other one, as smooth as baby skin. We declared that the last remaining wart would have to leave also!

#21 GOD had HEALED (1987)

There was a local auto salvage yard that I would periodically go to in order to purchase parts for my vehicles. The Lord put it into my heart to begin to go down there on a regular basis to witness to the owner and his son. This was a man who had a rough exterior, but on the inside I could sense a unique and tender-hearted person. He was the kind of man that I could relate with.

You see, I was raised in a very rough and tumble world. My grandpa, which was a large tell man, (I do not know what happened to me, I am only 5 feet 8 inches) was the original Texas kid! Grandpa was born in the late 1800s. Up until he died in 1973, he had a famous reputation. You did not mess with him. I still remember him with his cowboy hat, chewing tobacco in his mouth, and a large stogie in his hand.)

Back to the salvage yard. I would try to go there at least once a week to just chat with the owner, Dale. It really did not seem like I was getting anywhere with him spiritually. One day I received a phone call from him, which was highly unusual because he never called me. He seemed to be rather upset and distressed. He asked if I could come by and see him. I told him absolutely, and that I would be right down. When I got to his place of business, he began to share what was going on. He said that he had not been feeling very well lately, so he set up a doctor's appointment to go see what was wrong. When they were done with all of the tests and examinations, the prognosis was not very good. They informed

"GOD Healed Me HE Will Heal YOU"

him that he had cancer, and not just any cancer, but a very deadly form of cancer. I believe it was in his bone marrow and throughout his whole body. They told him there was no hope and that there was nothing they could do for him. They would not even give him chemotherapy, or radiation. When he was done telling me this tragic news, he asked me what he should do.

I could tell he was extremely serious. He was ready to do whatever it took. I told him he needed to give his heart to Jesus Christ. I said to him, "Put your hand into the hands of Jesus, and no matter what the outcome of this situation is, you need to walk with God." Right then and there, Dale gave his heart willingly and openly to Jesus Christ. (I could tell that his was a true conversion, and he immediately became faithful in coming to hear the Word at church.)

I laid my hands on him, and began to take authority over this spirit of cancer and death. I cursed it from its roots, and commanded it to go in the name of Jesus Christ of Nazareth. We proclaimed life and healing. I continued to pray as the Spirit of God spoke to my heart. Dale was in complete agreement.

When we were done, I told him, "God requires us to have prayer-supplication, and thanksgiving. Now you need to begin lifting your hands and praising God that you are completely healed and made whole, and thank God that the cancer is gone, and that you have been set free by the stripes of Jesus Christ and His precious blood." At that very moment, he felt something happen in his body. He told me he began to feel extremely good. He even went back to work. Then he set up an appointment to go see the doctors. Their prognosis was amazing! They said almost all of the cancer was completely gone. It was in complete remission. They had given Dale just a couple weeks to live, but now they were saying that the cancer was in total remission. This was to their total amazement!

I wish I could say this story ended well. It did in the sense that Dale is on the other side of eternity waiting for us now. I have seen this happen more times than I want to relate. God does wonderful miracles, and the medical world intrudes, stepping in to try to complete what God has begun. The doctors told Dale and his family that even though the cancer was in total remission, just in case, they would give chemo and radiation! They would not help him before because they said he was completely lost according to their estimates. But now that God had intervened, the medical world wanted to help Dale. The chemo and radiation took dale's life. I watched as his hair fell out, and he became a shadow of the man he was! I saw Dale in the last couple of hours before he died.

He said goodbye to me. He said he was tired of fighting, and he just wanted to go home to be with Jesus. I hugged him goodbye with tears rolling down my face. The next time I see Dale, it will be a glad reunion day in heaven.

#22 My Son Healed of an Incurable Affliction (1987)

When Daniel was little, he loved to put things in his mouth. While he was in the back seat of my sister's car, he found a can of DW 40. He was always inquisitive and nosey (and still is to this day). When he discovered the can of chemicals, his curiosity and the desire to put things in his mouth got the best of him. He sucked on the end and the cap popped off, so not only did he ingest the DW 40, but it also leaked all over him. By the time we realized what had happen, he was having a hard time breathing. I prayed over him, but he didn't seem to be getting any better. This chemical is not something to mess with!

Kathleen and I got someone to watch Michael while we took Daniel to our doctor right away. Informing the doctor what had happened, he strongly suggested x-rays, so we gave our approval. Lung problems have been a generational curse in my family, and I did not want Daniel to go through the same misery that I and other members of our family had gone through. My mother eventually died from medication related to her lung problems.

When the x-rays came back, the doctor's prognosis was not very encouraging. He showed us the x-rays. The chemicals he had gotten into were very dangerous. The x-ray showed that the chemicals were lining his lungs. Our doctor informed us that there was nothing that anybody could do for him. He also told us that he would always have breathing problems because of these chemicals in his lungs. We thanked him for his help, paid the medical bill, and left his office. From then on it was a fight for his life.

Many times late at night I would hear him struggling to breathe. Immediately, I would get up and take him into my arms, and begin to pray over him. I kept commanding the chemicals to come out of his lungs in the name of Jesus Christ of Nazareth. I would keep praying with him in the midst of it thanking, and praising God that he was healed, until he could be breathing normal, and then I would put him back to bed. This went on for many months. I began to notice that after each episode it would happen less and less. It has been over 20 years now since he has had an attack. Thank God, he's completely healed!

#23 How I was Healed of Hernia! (1988)

*I Kept Radically SHOVING my intestines back into where they belonged with my fingers.

Day after day we were putting up the steel of our church in 1986. We only had the use of a crane for a day during its construction. We had the crane handle all the heaviest beams. All the rest of the steel had to be carried and placed into position by hand. I'm not a very large man, as I only weighed about 140 pounds at the time. I was pulling and tugging, walking on steel beams, and balancing precariously on large steel Beams over my shoulder, and being carried up against my gut.

One day, as I was trying to put a heavy beam into place, I felt something rip in my lower abdomen. Later that day I noticed I had a large bulge. I had torn loose some stomach muscles. I had a hernia! I did not tell anyone. I found a quiet place and cried out to God. I laid my hands over the hernia, commanding it to go in the name of Jesus Christ of Nazareth. I went back to work because the building had to be put up. Every day I kept on lifting heavy steel. The hernia did not go away so I kept looking to God, trusting, and believing. The only one who became aware of the hernia was my wife. Honestly, I do not even remember telling her.

Why would I not tell anyone? It wasn't because I was afraid that people would have a poor opinion of me because I wasn't getting healed. I Have never worried in the least about people thinking I did not have faith. Faith is the substance that is or is not. You can fake faith, but then it's not faith. The Bible says if any man has faith, let him have it to himself. In my heart, there was nothing I needed to prove. You see, my confidence is in Jesus Christ, the Heavenly Father, and the Holy Ghost! If I have to go to the doctor, or use medication, it's nobody's business.

For over two years this hernia remained with me. The problem is I really was not aggressively dealing with it, but had gone into a state of passivity. I knew in my heart that it was time to deal with this monkey on my back. I began to speak to this hernia aggressively telling it that it was gone. Commanding my stomach lining to be made whole. The only problem is that the hernia had now come to the place of being almost Strangulated. It was quickened in my heart that I was going to have to get aggressive with this hernia. So, I would take my right hand and put my fingers against this hernia. Then I would SHOVE it back into where it belonged. As I SHOVED this hernia, I would be speaking to it. In the name of Jesus be healed! I commanded my intestines to stay where they belonged as I shoved up word.

"GOD Healed Me HE Will Heal YOU"

"Strangulated hernia. This is an irreducible hernia in which the entrapped intestine has its blood supply cut off. Pain is always present, followed quickly by tenderness and sometimes symptoms of bowel obstruction (nausea and vomiting). The affected person may appear ill with or without fever."

But Pastor Mike did you not know that you could die if this hernia got strangulated? YES, I knew this, but I also knew within my heart that By the Stripes of Jesus I Am Healed!

I cannot tell you how many times through the next two weeks that I kept SHOVING my intestines back up into my body with my fingertips. I would speak to it as Jesus told us to speak to the mountain. I told my stomach lining that it was healed. I told my intestines that they were healed. My body is the temple the Holy Ghost, and you have no right to be giving me any problems I would tell my intestines.

One Typical Night I Went to Bed And Got Up The Next Morning To A Miracle. The Hernia Was Completely Gone. Praise God, it has never come back! That has been over 30 years ago!

#24 Received Healing for a Busted Kneecap! (1988)

We had very heavy snowfall this particular winter. I owned an old John Dear snowmobile that I had made available to the local fire department if they ever needed my help. Eventually, they called me up during a terrible winter storm telling me that they had a heavy equipment operator that needed to be transported to Orrtanna.

He first needed to be picked up at his house and then delivered about 6 miles away. I informed them I would be more than willing to do this for them, especially because I love adventures. Actually, I am a snow addict. I can never get enough snow. The snowstorm and sleet had not yet abated and was raging in all its fury. I told my wife Kathleen that the fire department had called with a job for me to do. Mike to the rescue, or so I thought. I dressed up in all my winter trappings. I then went out and brushed the snow off my John Dear snowmobile and laid my hands on it, commanding it not to give me any problems. I should have prayed over myself first. I started the old machine up, revving the throttle as I headed out of the church parking lot. I turned to my right going down the deserted, main highway. There I was, having the time of my life and doing it for the fire department! Here I was doing about 50 miles an hour or faster, when I hit a section that was nothing but black ice.

The snowmobile's back end spun to the right out of control. I went flying through the air as it threw me for a lopper. I slammed my right kneecap extremely hard on the asphalt road. I felt my kneecap rip, break and tear as I kept sliding down the road for quite a distance. The snowmobile had continued on its way, spinning out of control. The snowmobile itself eventually stopped because my hand was no longer cranking the throttle. Fortunately, it was not damaged because there was nothing but snow in every direction. There I was, lying on the road in the snow and freezing wind, clutching my busted up knee, alone and in tremendous pain! Immediately, I cried out to Jesus and repented for being so stupid and for not using Godly wisdom.

My theology is that almost everything that goes wrong in my life is usually my own stupid fault. Even if the devil is involved in it, it is most likely because I first opened the door for him. After I was done repenting and confessing to the Lord, I went aggressively after my healing. I commanded my kneecap to be put back into its normal condition in the name of Jesus Christ of Nazareth. I commanded every broken part of it to be made whole.

"GOD Healed Me HE Will Heal YOU"

You see, I could grab my patella and move it all around. It was no longer attached to my knee. It seemed to have become completely disconnected, no longer restrained by its associated ligaments.

Probably at this juncture, most people would have called it quits when it comes to completing the mission they set out on. But that is not my mode of operation. If I declared that I was healed then I needed to act upon it. I discovered a truth a long time ago, God cannot lie! So, I slowly crawled back over to my snow machine and pulled myself back into the seat. I painfully swung my right leg over the seat into its proper position. At that very moment, wave after wave of pain overwhelmed me. Years of experience walking in faith, however, caused me to declare that I am healed in the name of Jesus. In the name of Jesus, I am healed. I opened the throttle and proceeded on the way to pick up the equipment operator. I kept proclaiming the truth.

On the way, there were a lot of areas where my snowmobile just would not go. The snow was way too deep in some areas to go or the road was flooded with water in others. The storm had dumped a combination of rain, ice and snow. One would need a boat to go through some of the areas where I went. Admittedly, at times I took chances that I should not have taken. I would accelerate to a high speed and just zip across the flooded areas. The back end of the snowmobile would begin to sink as if I wasn't going to make it. But, I would constantly revert back to the old trusted declaration: In the name of Jesus, in the name of Jesus, in the name of Jesus, I will make it. There are a lot of wonderful messages preached on faith but that's not what wins the victory. It is when the Word has been quickened in your heart that you know, that you know, that you know, that you know that God and His Word are true.

I cannot describe to you enough the immense pain and agony that I was going through, yet I did not merely think that I was healed, I knew that I was healed! Faith is not thinking, hoping, or wishing. It is knowing that you know, that you know, that you know. I finally reached my first destination. The township worker saw me pull up outside of his house. As he came to the machine, he could not see my face because of my helmet and my ski mask. I did not tell him that I had an accident and possibly shattered my kneecap. I do not adhere to bragging about the devil or his shenanigans, lies or deceptions. This was no little man that I had to carry on the back of my machine either. He mounted up and we were on our way. It took major faith to keep on going. We had to take numerous detours before I finally got him to the big earthmover that he was tasked to operate. He jumped off my snowmobile and thanked me for the ride. I told him it was no problem as I opened up the throttle and headed home.

This time, I decided to take a different route because the last route was so bad. It took all the faith that I could muster to get back to the parsonage. I was cold, wet, tired and completely overwhelmed with pain from the shattered knee. When I got home, I just kept thanking God that I was healed. During the next couple of days, I refused to pamper my leg. I did not put any ice or heat upon it. I did not take any kind of medication or painkillers. I did not call anyone asking them to please pray for me and to believe God for my healing. I know this may seem extremely stupid, but I knew in my heart that I was healed. It has got to be in your heart! My head, my body and my throbbing, busted kneecap were all telling me that I was not healed, but let God's Word be true and every symptom a lie. When the next Sunday rolled around, the roads were clear enough for people to make it to church.

During that time, you might have called me Hop-Along Cassidy because of the way that I was walking. I do not deny the problem, but I sure as heaven denied the right for it to exist! One of our parishioners, who was a nurse, saw me limping badly. She asked me what happened and I told her. She informed me that this was a major problem. She tried to explain to me in medical terms exactly what she thought I had done to my knee. Medically, in order to reattach and repair my patella, I would have to endure at least one major surgical procedure. She recounted to me that she

"GOD Healed Me HE Will Heal YOU"

had once had a similar injury although it was nowhere near as bad as mine. She went on to elaborate that even after an extensive operation, her knee was still giving her major problems. I thanked her for this information and went back to trusting and believing that by the stripes of Jesus Christ, I was healed.

I sure as heaven was not going to let go or to give up on God's promises. I wrestled with this situation day after day, commanding my knee to be healed and to function as God had designed it to do. When the pain would overwhelm me, I would tell it to shut up, be quiet and work! When it seemed like my leg would not carry me, I would command it to be strong in the name of Jesus. This went on for well over a month. One morning I crawled out of bed and my knee cap was perfectly healed. You would think that when the healing manifested that I would begin to sing, shout and dance, but I did not and I do not! You see I had already done all of my rejoicing in advance because I believe that the minute I prayed, I received!!!

CHAPTER SIX

#25 Mafia call girl touched by the Holy Ghost (1988)

One day I received a phone call from a woman who had visited our church. She was a very staunch Catholic, who had given her heart to Christ. She asked if I could possibly help them in a very difficult situation with their daughter. They began to explain to me that their daughter, who was a very beautiful woman, had at some point been caught up with the Mafia. She literally had become a call girl for the Mafia. In the mist of her wild activities with the Mafia, she had become completely cut off from the rest of her family. She had put the whole family through tremendous pain and suffering because of her activities.

The day came when out of the blue they received a phone call from her. She informed them that she had been having some difficulties with her body, and that after physical examinations it was discovered that she had incurable cancer. She was in such bad condition that she could no longer work as a call girl.

As I listened to the mother, I could tell that her heart was filled with great distress, and yet there was an undercurrent of anger. She was very angry with her daughter and what she had put them through. Now they were calling me because she was finally at the very door of death itself. The medical world had done all they could for her, but there was no hope. I think in the mind of this young lady's parents I might come and do last rights like a Catholic priest. They were hoping if I could come over as soon as possible, because she was that close to death. At any moment she was going to step over the edge into eternity. I informed them that I would be right over, with my wife.

"GOD Healed Me HE Will Heal YOU"

We live West of Gettysburg, but where they lived was approximately 22 miles east of us in a town called Hanover. I knew in my heart they simply wanted me to get her to pray a prayer of salvation, and then the blessings, and basically then they would say their goodbyes. I knew right away we were going to have a problem because I just do not operate that way. I know in my heart that there is nothing impossible with God, and he likes to take the most difficult situations, turn them around because of his great love, and because of who HE is.

When we arrived at the house the mother and father, brothers, relatives were waiting. It felt like a funeral home. They were expecting her to die at any moment. Everything was arranged for her death! They informed us that she was nothing but skin and bones. She was excreting black and ugly fluids from her mouth, and her private parts. They just wanted me to realize that her life on earth was over. Basically what they were saying is just pray with her, so we can bury her, making sure that she would never go back into her old lifestyle. What I am sharing with you is not me being critical of them, just knowing exactly in my heart what they were saying. Their hearts were filled with great fear that if God would raise her up off the bed of death she would go back to her old lifestyle.

They lived in an old two-story house, and their daughter was in a bedroom on the 2nd floor. As they were sharing with me their concerns, desires, and exactly what they wanted me to do I simply listened. I did not make any kind of statement or commitments to them, promises or insinuations of what I would do. I had not come to please them, but to hear from heaven for this young lady. I thanked them for all of their information letting them know that now I would like to see their daughter.

My wife and I walked up the stairs, turned down the hallway, and went to the room they told us she was in. We knocked softly 1st, and not hearing a response, we entered. There she was, a dark haired, at one time, beautiful 26-year-old girl. She was lying in her bed with her eyes deep sunk, but wide open. The terrible smell of death was in the room. There was a sheet covering her body, but it was easy to tell that she was nothing but skin and bones. I introduced myself with my wife, telling her that I was a pastor and we had come to pray for her. It turns out that she was quite alert and responsive.

The very first thing I did was share with her the reality of Christ, and the difference he had made in my life. At one time I had lived a very unseemly and wicked existence. I had ran with a gang outside of Chicago, and done things that I was extremely ashamed of, but through the precious blood of Jesus Christ I had been forgiven. Now Christ himself lived within me, having transformed and made me into a brand-new person.

My wife also spoke for a while to her, talking softly and tenderly about the love of Christ. I perceive the spirit of God was working on her for her eyes filled with tears. We asked her if she would like to commit her heart and her life to Jesus Christ. And with a whisper she said yes.

We immediately had a witness within our hearts that she truly did accept Christ as her Lord and Saviour, and that she was now born again. Now at this point I had a choice to make; was I going to let her die and go home to be with Jesus, or would I share with her the reality that Christ could raise her from the bed of death? I could not walk away from her without telling her that Christ would make her whole. My wife and I began to share the truth that Jesus is the great physician. In his earthly life he had healed everybody, because it is the will of God for all to be saved and to be healed. As I began to speak the truth of divine healing, and that by the stripes of Jesus we are made whole, I perceived that faith was flooding into her soul. We asked her if she would allow us to ask God to raise her up off the bed of death. She wholeheartedly agreed with that request. We laid our hands on her in the mighty name of Jesus Christ of Nazareth, commanding the spirit of cancer and death to come out of her. We commanded her bodily organs to be restored and to be made whole.

The room was filled with a wonderful sweet presence of Jesus Christ. After we had prayed for her we encouraged her to

"GOD Healed Me HE Will Heal YOU"

begin to feed herself the truth of God's word. We encouraged her to feed herself by good godly ministers on the TV (there is one in her room) that would teach and preach Divine healing. We gave her a list of certain ministers that we knew who were on TV who strongly and boldly declares that healing is for today, and for everyone. We also informed her that we would be back as much as possible in order to continue to speak life over her. We would also be bringing teaching materials, and cassette tapes that would encourage her in her faith in Christ. Before we left the room, my wife and I perceived that there was already a wonderful improvement in her body. When we entered the room it had the smell of death, but now the very presence of God, almost a divine light, had entered the room. We told her goodbye, letting her know that we would be back soon.

My wife and I went downstairs to see the family. As we came down the stairs they were all looking up at us, wanting to know what had happened. I informed them with great joy that she had given her heart to Christ. I also informed them that we had prayed for her to be raised up from the bed of death. The minute I told them this, I sensed hatred coming from them towards my wife and I for praying and believing God for her healing. They truly did not want her to be raised up, because they really thought that she would go back to being a call girl for the Mafia. From that point forward there was great animosity in them against us. Every time we would come to their house, we could tell that they did not want us there. There are many times when they would not even speak to us as we came to see their daughter.

My wife and I began to visit two or three times every week. She immediately began to get better. She was eating, sitting up, and talking more. Her countenance was completely different. When we would visit her we would discuss the different biblical principles. She would tell us the ministers that she was watching, and how exciting the word of God was. In her bedroom there was the presence of heaven, but downstairs in the mist of her family was the presence of hell. She told us that she knew her parents were extremely upset with us because we were standing with her for her complete healing.

One Sunday morning we were pleasantly surprised as she walked into our church underneath her own strength. Yes there were still some symptoms of cancer in her, but she was doing better every day. About two weeks after her visit, we went to see her at her parents' house. When we walked into the house, the atmosphere was not just anger, but there was also once again the sense of death hanging in the air. I hate to say this, but they almost reminded me of buzzards hanging over some animal who had just been hit on the road, waiting for the animal to die. They really did not say much to us, so we simply went up the stairs. When we entered into this precious sister's room we were shocked to see her lying in her bed, with death once again hanging over the top of her. We asked her what was going on.

She informed us that it would be best for her to die because her parents and family members were so tormented over the thought that she might go back to her old lifestyle. Day by day they had been fighting her, attacking her, and nagging her. My wife and I looked at each other, we knew what we had to do. I told her that we had a spare bedroom in our house, and that we would gladly take her in. We would stand with her in faith, until she was completely restored. And we would disciple her in the things of God. She thanked us with all the sincerity of our heart, but told us that she could not do this. She informed us that her family already hated us for encouraging her to live, and that if we would take her into our house there would be such hatred in their hearts, that they would never forgive us. She basically said goodbye to us right then and there. Our hearts were filled with great sorrow, as we hugged her and as we said our last goodbyes. That was the last time we saw her alive.

It wasn't very long before she had passed on to eternity. They did ask me do the funeral, but even in that service there was still great animosity in the air. I tried to speak as much love and comfort that I could to these tormented people, who had allowed the devil to take them captive in their thoughts and emotions. They did not believe that Christ was big enough to transform the heart of their daughter.

What is so sad is they did not see that she had literally

become a new creation. Love emanated from her for God and for people. The girl we had gone to visit, had literally died on that first visit. God had raised up a new person, a brand-new creation, but those who were close to her could not see it. Our hearts were sad over the fact that she passed on, and yet we rejoice with the fact that we will see her again on the other side. Not as a call girl for the Mafia, but a brand-new creation, a glorious holy, and wonderful woman of God.

#26 Dangerous Attack of Conjunctivitis (1993)

I am sharing this story in order to help you to understand how to take a hold of your healing. You see John 10:10 says that the thief comes to steal, kill and destroy. It tells us in the book of James to submit ourselves to God, resist the devil, and he will flee from us. The very minute that any type of physical affliction attack our bodies is the very moment that we need to take a hold of God, and then come against the enemy of our souls. ***Our bodies are the temples of the Holy Ghost, and the enemy has no right to afflict them.***

One of the brothers of the church where I pastor went with me to the Philippines. We were ministering in the province of Samar, which is one of the five provinces of the Philippines. It takes an airplane ride from Manila, and then transferring to ground vehicles. The trip is rather long, tiring and challenging. Not including the fact that we are in the territory of the New People's Army, which is an anti-government communist movement. Believe me when I tell you that they will kill you in a heartbeat.

When we finally arrived at our destination, the Filipinos we were working with were waiting for us. The local pastors and believers had already prepared the way for us to hold crusades in different towns and villages. In the natural they really did not need us because they are all walking in the realities of God. To some extent we Americans are like White Elephants in that we draw a crowd. We do not have any more of the Holy Spirit or the word of God than they do.

As we were on our way for the first set of meetings all of our team including myself was attacked with Conjunctivitis, commonly called Pinkeye. Conjunctivitis is caused by a virus that can be dangerous in two ways. First, the person with the infection can lose some of their vision; in severe cases they can totally lose their eyesight. This could be for a short time, or it could be permanent. Second, the infection can spread very rapidly, and is highly infectious. People with "pink eye" often get conjunctivitis germs on their hands by rubbing their eyes, then leave the germs on the objects they touch.

The first sign of this affliction is that your eyes begin to feel dry and irritated. And then it gets to the point where it literally feels like someone has grabbed a handful of sand and shoved it into your eyes, grinding your eyeballs slowly with the sand. The whites of your eyes eventually turn pink, and can become blood red when it's really bad.

The very minute my eyes began to become irritated, I found a quiet place of prayer. I simply spoke to my heavenly Father thanking Him for what Jesus had done for me when He had received the stripes upon his back. After meditating upon these realities for a while, it was time to take my authority that Christ has given to all believers. I spoke the name of Jesus to this affliction, commanding it to go, now, now, now in the name of Jesus Christ of Nazareth. No ifs, ands or buts! And then I followed through with thanksgiving, praising and thanking God that I was healed. Not that I was going to be healed, but that I was healed, now! From that moment forward it did not matter how I felt, or looked. I knew that I knew that I knew that I was healed. I just kept thanking God and praising God quietly, and in my heart.

I went on my way rejoicing even though it did not feel any different, or look any different. Not one more word came out of my mouth to anyone about this affliction, or how terrible my eyes felt. Within less than two days all of the symptoms were gone.

I'm sorry to say that this was not the case for the rest of the team. A lot of these precious people were going through terrible irritation. The brother I had brought with me began to get much worse. Eventually the white of his eyes turned blood red. I knew in my heart that if we did not do something he could go blind.

This continued for over a week, when he finally came to me telling me that he had to get back to America. I have learned a long time ago to not be critical of people, but to work with them where they are at. He told me that I could continue the meetings, but he was leaving. I informed them that I would go with him making sure he was going to get back home. He was my responsibility as his pastor and also the spiritual authority of these meetings.

Of course my precious Filipino brothers were slightly upset because there were meetings that still needed to be fulfilled. I informed them that I was sorry but my first responsibility was to this brother, and that the Holy Ghost would move through them, and speak through them.

In order to cut our trip short, it was going to take faith to get on the plane earlier than when we were scheduled to leave. And we also had to believe that we were not going to be stopped by customs because of the highly contagious affliction in his eyes. All the way home he kept dark sunglasses on. Through a series of miracles, we were able to board a plane early and get back to America.

The infection that he had picked up in the Philippines did not leave him without medical help. Thank God he did not lose his eyes. Jesus always worked with us where we are at. My position is one of being there for people no matter what. We help, pray and encourage where we can. If we do not see a miracle we simply keep our eyes on Jesus. If we fall short, we just determine in our heart to get back up and keep on going. If I run into situations where it does not seem like I can receive healing, I just go deeper into God, his word, and his will for my life. *God will never let you down!*

#27 Crippled Women Healed in Great Brittan (1993)

I've had the wonderful experience of going to Great Britain (five times) from Wales and Scotland. I had the privilege of seeing many miracles and wonders on these five journeys. At one particular meeting where I was conducting a citywide healing service, there was a very heavyset lady in a wheelchair on the front row. This meeting was not held in a church, but it was a community center so that other churches would come together.

After I was finished ministering the Word of God on the subject of healing, the Holy Ghost quickened me to go over and lay my hands upon this lady. I had no idea what was wrong with her. As I laid my hands upon her, I commanded her to be healed and made whole in the name of Jesus Christ of Nazareth. When I was finished praying and commanding her to be healed, I told her to get up out of her wheelchair and walk whenever she was ready. Then I took two or three steps back away from her. I saw faith flashing in her eyes! She began to push her large body up out of her wheelchair. When she was finally standing up on her feet, she began to move her feet forward one little step at a time. She was walking! It really did not seem that spectacular to me, but the congregation was amazed.

After the service, I discovered what had happened to her. She had been in a terrible car accident ten years previously, and both of her legs were extremely damaged to the point that they were useless. One leg was so mangled that the doctors had insisted on it

"GOD Healed Me HE Will Heal YOU"

being amputated. This precious sister refused to let them take her leg. She had not walked since the accident and now she was walking. Glory to God!

> *Jesus answered and said unto them, Go and shew John again those things which ye do hear and see: The blind receive their sight, and the lame walk, the lepers are cleansed, and the deaf hear, the dead are raised up, and the poor have the gospel preached to them (Matthew 11:4-5).*

CHAPTER SEVEN

#28 Brand-new Liver (1993)

One day I had to go visit one of my parishioners in the Gettysburg Hospital. When I make these visitations, many times I will wear a minister's collar because it is a recognized symbol of religious authority. It's amazing how a little piece of white plastic can have such an effect on medical professionals, this also includes policemen and others in natural authority. When I put on a minister's collar I look almost like a Catholic priest.

Many times through the years I have walked into a hospital room, with doctors and nurses present. In most situations, they will ask me to wait outside until they are done. But the Scripture says be as wise as the serpent, as harmless as a dove. So I go in as one in authority. When I do this the doctors themselves submit to my religious authority. I ask the doctors and nurses kindly to leave so I can minister to the person. Surprisingly they bow their heads, walking out of the room.

One day I walked into a man's room who I did not know. I asked him what his problem was. He told me that his liver was completely shot, and that he was dying. I perceived in my heart that it was because of alcoholism. I told him that I would like to pray for him, and ask if that was possible. He agreed to my request. I laid my hands on him, commanding in the name of Jesus Christ for the spirit of infirmity to come out. And then I spoke into him a brand-new liver, in the name of Jesus Christ of Nazareth! I do not speak loud. I do not have to because I know my Authority in Christ, when I am submitted to the authority of Christ! I do not pray real long prayers, or even dozens of scriptures. The Word is already in my heart! Now believe me when I tell you that if I

"GOD Healed Me HE Will Heal YOU"

wanted to pray real long prayers in those situations I easily could. I could stand over the person and quote whole books of the Bible by memory. When you are moving in the realm of faith none of these things are necessary. Many times it is obvious that people are trying to work up faith. If you study the life of Jesus and his ministry he never spent a long time praying, or speaking over people. The long hours of prayer, and speaking the word was done in private, when he was up on the mountain.

When I was done, I simply said goodbye, and out the door I went. I was to go see another sick person. It was three years later when I finally discovered what happened on that particular day. One of the members of my congregation was down on the streets of Gettysburg witnessing to those he met. He ran into this particular gentleman who was dying because he needed a new liver. This particular man said: I know who your pastor is! The parishioner asked: how do you know my pastor? He said: three years ago I was dying with a bad liver. Your pastor walked in, and laid his hands on me commanding me to have a brand-new liver. And God gave me a brand-new liver!

Matthew 10:8 Heal the sick, cleanse the lepers, raise the dead, cast out devils: freely ye have received, freely give.

#29 The deliverance of Sarah from TS (1994)

Tourette syndrome (TS) is a neurological disorder characterized by repetitive, stereotyped, involuntary movements and vocalizations called tics.

Three months before school was out in 1994 I received a phone call from a husband and wife from Carlisle Pennsylvania. They called, asking if we could possibly help them. They had been watching my TV program which was aired over their local TV station. They knew from my messages on TV, that we had a

Christian school. They had a daughter who was 10 years old, who desperately needed help. Not only did she have tics syndrome, but she had major emotional problems.

The principle of the public school that she attended was demanding they place her in to a mental institution. She was completely uncontrollable. Whenever they would try to discipline her, she would run from them, many times ending up in the parking lot, crawling under the cars. One time when she was in the principal's office, Sarah got so angry, that she completely wiped out this office. They told me that she had gone completely berserk trashing everything in her sight. The principal of the school could not handle it anymore. The only other option this couple had was to see if somebody would take her into their school. Our school was over 30 miles away from where they lived, but they were willing to drive it every day. I told them that I would pray about it to see what the Lord spoke to me. I truly felt in my heart that we could help this young lady. A meeting was set up to meet the parents with their daughter Sarah.

    I like to always pray before I make any commitments. I sought the Lord about this terrible situation with their daughter. As I spoke face-to-face with the parents, and with meeting Sarah for the first time, I perceived in my heart we could help her. First I told them that if we were going to help Sarah for the next three months, they would have to allow us to do what we felt needed to be done. The very first thing that they would need to do was to take Sarah off all mind altering drugs, which the public school had put her on. This is always one of our requirements for a child to come to our school. From 1985, up to this moment, in our school we never allowed any mind altering drugs. In every situation we have seen God do marvellous things in a student's life.

    The second thing I told the parents is that we would want them not to hang around at all at the school, once they drop their daughter off. I perceived by the spirit of God that a lot of Sarah's problem was that she was using her condition as a way to get attention from her mother and father. This proved to be correct, because every time her mother came to pick her up, the tics

"GOD Healed Me HE Will Heal YOU"

became much worse. When she first came to our school her head would shake back and forth very violently all day long. It was extremely painful to watch. I had a meeting with my teachers informing them that they were not to lift their voice, or yell at Sarah for any reason. We were not going to put her in a situation that would stir up the devils that were manifesting through her.

Many so-called Christians, especially the spirit filled ones, would have been trying to cast the devils out of her the minute they saw her, because they would have thought she was demon possessed. Granted, there were devils at work, but she was not possessed. She was oppressed, depressed and at times obsessed. People who do not have a lot of wisdom immediately try to cast devils out without getting the mind of Christ.

The spirit of God literally told me what we needed to do. Every morning when her mother dropped her off, I would take her with one of the female teachers of the school into an office. I would speak very softly to Sarah, telling her that we would like to pray with her before the beginning of the day. I would simply speak in a very soft voice over her that which was the will of God. This prayer would usually only be about five minutes long. Then I would tell her that she was going to have a wonderful day. Off to her class she would go. We did not treat her any different than the other students. Through the day if they began to have problems with her, they would simply send someone to get me.

Once again we would take her into an office (with a lady teacher) and I would gently pray over her in the name of Jesus Christ. I also came against the demonic spirits that was causing the tics syndrome. I never got loud, authoritative, or weird. I would simply take authority over them, in a quiet gentle voice. Immediately there was a wonderful change in Sarah. Every day she was getting better. Not only did the tics syndrome cease eventually, but she became an A+ student. It was obvious to me at the beginning that Sarah was a brilliant girl, who was not being challenged at the school she attended.

By the end of the three months, Sarah was completely free.

She was a happy, smiling, hard-working A+ student. We could not have asked for a better young girl. I am sorry to say that at the end of those three months we never saw Sarah or her parents again. I guess they had gotten what they needed, and off they went. This is very typical in my experience.

When the next school year rolled around, I received a very strange phone call one day from the Carlisle school district. The principal was on the phone wanting to talk to me. When I got on the phone with this principal, who was a lady, she asked me a question with a tone of absolute surprise and wonder. She said to me: what in the world did you do with Sarah? She is completely changed!

I said to this principal, who was over a large school district, "What we did with Sarah you're not going to be able to do!" I said to her: we began to pray over her very gently, every day, consistently in the name of Jesus Christ. You could literally hear a pin drop for the next couple moments. The next thing I heard was, OH, okay, goodbye! The principal hung up the phone!

#30 God gave her a NEW HEART (1994)

A precious sister in the Lord (sister VI) ended up in the Chambersburg hospital with an extremely dangerous heart condition. I went to the Hospital. I walked into her room. She had all kinds of medical equipment hooked up to her. It looked extremely serious. The spirit of compassion was quickened in me, and I laid my hands on her. I commanded her HEART to be healed in the name of Jesus Christ of Nazareth. After we spoke for a while I left her. At that moment it did not seem as if there had been any change in her whatsoever.

"GOD Healed Me HE Will Heal YOU"

She shared her testimony with me later. The minute I walked out of the Room the equipment that was monitoring her began to sound alarms. The nurses came running. She told them everything was okay. That her pastor had prayed for her. And God had healed her. They looked and treated her like she was crazy! They put her through all kinds of test, over and over they tested her. She kept telling them God had done a miracle and given her a NEW HEART! After many test they had to finally admit she was completely healed. All praise and glory to God!!!

The Spirit of the Lord is upon me, because he hath anointed me to preach the gospel to the poor; he hath sent me to heal the brokenhearted, to preach deliverance to the captives, and recovering of sight to the blind, to set at liberty them that are bruised, to preach the acceptable year of the Lord (Luke 4:18-19).

#31 I Overcame Colon Cancer without doctors! (2003)

I began to experience some very disturbing symptoms in my body. I will not go into all the details but there were approximately nine different physical symptoms. One of the symptoms was almost every time I had a bowel movement, it looked as if all my innards were coming out. During this 3-month period of time, I was so sick sometimes that I thought that I was going to die at any moment. My normal course of action is that the minute my body begins to manifest any kind of sickness or disease, I immediately command it to go in the Name of Jesus Christ of Nazareth!

These symptoms simply refuse to leave. I made a list of everything that was happening in my body and then I looked these symptoms up on the internet. Every one of them pointed to colon cancer. I had gone through a similar fight of faith a number of years previously, with what seemed to be prostate cancer. Once again, I took hold of the Word of God. I boldly declared to the devil, myself and the spiritual world that I would live and not die. I cried out to Jesus for His mercy and His grace in the midst of this fight of faith. This fight was almost overwhelming and excruciating at times!

For these three months I continued with this fight. I spoke to the symptoms commanding them to go. I kept praising, thanking and worshiping God that I was healed; no ifs, ands or buts. I declared boldly that the devil is a liar. For three months every day, all day at times, declaring what God said about me. I did not invite anybody else to stand with me in this fight of faith. Most people, if they would have known what I was going through, would have pronounced me dead and gone.

Believe it or not there are actually people who call themselves Christians who would have rejoiced in my death. Yes, they would have been telling people to pray, but there would have been more negative comments, than agreement with the reality of God's Word. ***By His stripes we were healed***! If I were healed, then I was healed, and if I was healed, then I am healed, and if I am healed, then I is healed!

For three long months I stood and fought by faith. Many nights and days walking the floor of our church sanctuary praising God that I was healed, resisting the spirit of fear. One day I woke up and all of the symptoms had disappeared, praise God. And they have never come back. Thank you, Jesus,!!! I had a friend in the medical world that sat down and discussed the situation with me. He asked me for all the specific symptoms that I had. When I finished he told me that without any doubt I had had colon cancer. Did you notice the word, I had had, but no longer! Praise the Lord.

"GOD Healed Me HE Will Heal YOU"

#32 Pastor Healed of Terrible Fungus (2009)

My wife and I were ministering at a church in the Harrisburg, Pennsylvania area. I had finished ministering the message that God had laid on my heart, and now I was beginning to move in the gifts of the Holy Spirit. God began to confirm His word with wonderful signs and wonders. The word of knowledge, wisdom and discerning of spirits were being manifested as I surrendered and yielded to the Spirit of God. New wine began to flow as people were being touched by the Holy Ghost. As I was finishing up with one of the people we were praying for, I looked over at the pastor who was sitting on the front row of chairs with his wife.

This pastor is a rather large man, in height and weight. The Holy Spirit drew my attention to his feet. Because he is also involved in the farming industry, he was wearing a heavy duty pair of shoes. As I was looking at the shoes, all of a sudden I could see right through them. It actually shocked me to some extent. I could see very clearly his feet and toes. This experience was so real that it pulled me right over to him. I stood in front of this pastor looking at his feet, with a look of surprise on my face. I pointed right down at his feet, stating: what is going on with your toes? He said: what? I repeated my question: what is going on with your toes?

I could see that they were completely covered in fungus! I saw that even the nails of his toes were gone, or completely covered in black, yellow nasty fungus. I told him, fungus! Your toes and your feet are completely covered in fungus! He answered and said: yes, they have been like that for many years. When I used to play football (must have been about forty years earlier) somehow I contracted this fungus, and I have never been able to get rid of it.

I fell to my knees right then and there, putting my hands on his shoes. I spoke to the fungus on his toes, and feet, commanding that in the name of Jesus Christ it had to go. I told the spirit of infirmity to leave his feet now in the name of Jesus. As I spoke the word of God, I knew in my heart by a gift of faith, and the gift of healing that he was healed. I told him, it's gone. In the name of Jesus it is gone, and you are healed. At that moment I got up off the floor and continued to minister to others by the spirit of God.

About a month later I was back in this man's church ministering. I asked him: brother, how is your feet? He told me the fungus was all gone, and that after all those years he was now free. Jesus Christ, by the gifts of the Holy Ghost, had revealed this need, and caused him to be completely healed.

CHAPTER EIGHT

#33 Broken Foot Instantly Healed (1996)

One day I had to climb our 250 foot AM radio tower in order to change the light bulb on the main beacon. However, in order to climb the tower, I had to first find the keys; which I never did. Since I could not find the keys to get the fence open, I did the next best thing—I simply climbed over the fence.

This idea turned out not to be such a wonderful idea after all! With all of my climbing gear hanging from my waist, I climbed the fence to the very top. At this point, my rope gear became entangled in the fencing. As I tried to get free, I lost my balance and fell backwards off the fence. Trying to break my fall, I got my right foot down underneath me. I hit the ground with my foot being turned on its side and I felt something snap in the ankle. I knew instantly I had a broken foot, my ankle.

Most normal people would have climbed back over the fence, go set up a doctor's appointment, have their foot x rayed, and then placed into a cast. But I am not a normal-thinking person, at least according to the standards of the modern day church. When I broke my foot, I followed my routine of confessing my stupidity to God, and asking Him to forgive me for my stupidity. Moreover, then I spoke to my foot and commanded it to be healed in the name of Jesus Christ of Nazareth. When I had finished speaking to my foot, commanding it to be healed, and then praising and thanking God for the healing, there seem to be no change what so ever in its condition.

The Scripture that came to my heart was where Jesus declared, ***"The kingdom of heaven suffereth violence, and the violent take*** *it by force!"* Based completely upon this scripture, I decided to climb the tower by faith, with a broken foot mind you. Please do not misunderstand, my foot hurt so bad I could hardly stand it. And yet, I had declared that I believed I was healed.

There were three men watching me as I took the Word of God by faith. I told them what I was about to do, and they looked at me like as if I had lost my mind. I began to climb the 250-foot tower, one painful step at a time. My foot hurt so bad that I was hyperventilating within just twenty to thirty feet up the tower. It literally felt like I was going to pass out from shock at any moment. Whenever I got to the point of fainting, I would connect my climbing ropes to the tower, stop and take a breather, crying out to Jesus to help me. It seemed to take me forever to get to the top.

Even so, I finally did reach the very top of the tower and replaced the light bulb that had gone out. Usually I can come down that tower within 10 minutes, because I would press my feet against the tower rods, and then slide down, just using my hands and arms to lower myself at a very fast pace. However, in this situation, my foot could not handle the pressure of being pushed up against the steel. Consequently, I had to work my way down very slowly. After I was down, I slowly climbed over the fence one more time. I hobbled my way over to my vehicle, and drove up to the church office. The men who had been watching this unfold, were right behind me.

I hobbled my way into the front office; which is directly across the street from the radio tower. I informed the personnel that I had broken my foot, showing them my black and blue, extremely swollen foot. It did not help that I had climbed with it! I told them that I was going home to rest. At the same time, however, I told them that I believed I was healed.

Going to my house, which is directly across from the main office of the church parking lot, I made my way slowly up the stairs to our bedroom. I found my wife in the bedroom putting away our clothes. Slowly and painfully I pulled the shoe and sock off of the broken foot. What a mess! It was fat, swollen, black and blue all over. I put a pillow down at the end of the bed, and carefully pulled myself up onto the bed. Lying on my back, I tenderly placed my broken, black and blue, swollen foot onto the pillow. No matter how I positioned it, the pain did not cease. I just laid there squirming, moaning and sighing.

As I was lying there trying to overcome the shock that kept hitting my body, I heard the audible voice of God. He said to me: "What are you doing in bed? God really got my attention when I heard him with my natural ears. My wife would testify that she heard nothing. Immediately in my heart I said: Lord I'm just resting. Then He spoke to my heart with the still small voice very clearly, Do you always rest at this time of day? No, Lord, I replied. (It was about 3 o'clock in the afternoon)

He spoke to my heart again and said: I thought you said you were healed?

At that very moment the gift of faith exploded inside of me. I said, "Lord, I am healed! Immediately, I pushed myself up off of the bed, grabbed my sock and shoe, and struggled to put them back on. What a tremendous struggle it was! My foot was so swollen that it did not want to go into the shoe. My wife was watching me as I fought to complete this task. You might wonder what my wife was doing this whole time as I was fighting this battle of faith. She was doing what she always does, just watching me and shaking her head. I finally got the shoe on my swollen, black and blue foot. I put my foot down on the floor and began to put my body weight upon it. When I did, I almost passed out. At that moment, a holy anger exploded on the inside of me. I declared out loud, "I am healed in the name of Jesus Christ of Nazareth!" With that declaration, I took my right (broken) foot, and slammed it down to the floor as hard as I possibly could.

When I did that, I felt the bones of my foot break even more. Like the Fourth of July, an explosion of blue, purple, red, and white, black exploded in my brain and I passed out. I came to lying on my bed. Afterward, my wife informed me that every time I passed out, it was for about ten to twenty seconds. The moment I came to, I jumped right back up out of bed. The gift of faith was working in me mightily. I got back up and followed the same process again, "In the name of Jesus Christ of Nazareth I am healed," and slammed my foot down once more as hard as I could! For a second time, I could feel the damage in my foot increasing. My mind was once again wrapped in an explosion of colors and pain as I blacked out.

When I regained consciousness, I immediately got up once again, repeating the same process. After the third time of this happening I came to with my wife leaning over the top of me. I remember my wife saying as she looked at me, "You're making me sick. I can't watch you do this." She promptly walked out of our bedroom, and went downstairs.

The fourth time I got up declaring, "In the name of Jesus Christ of Nazareth I am healed," and slammed my foot even harder! Once more, multiple colors of intense pain hit my brain. I passed out again! I got up the fifth time, angrier than ever. This was not a demonic or proud anger. This was a divine gift of violent I-will-not-take-no-for-an-answer type of faith. I slammed my foot down the fifth time, "In the name of Jesus Christ of Nazareth I am healed!" The minute my foot slammed into the floor, for the fifth time, the power of God hit my foot. I literally stood there under the quickening power of God, and watched my foot shrink and become normal. All of the pain was completely and totally gone. I pulled back my sock, and watched the black and blue in my foot disappear to normal flesh color. I was healed! Praise God, I was made whole! I went back to the office, giving glory to the Lord and showing the staff my healed foot.

"GOD Healed Me HE Will Heal YOU"

#34 God Healed my son from rabies! (2000)

When my son Daniel was 16 years old in 2000, he brought home a baby raccoon. He wanted to keep this raccoon as a pet. Immediately, people began to inform me that this was illegal. I further learned that in order to have a raccoon in Pennsylvania, one had to purchase one from someone who was licensed by the state to sell them. The reason for this was because of the high rate of rabies carried among them. But stubbornness rose up in my heart against what they were telling me, and I ignored sound logic.

You see, I had a raccoon when I was a child. Her mother had been killed on the highway and left behind a litter of her little ones. I had taken one of the little ones and bottle-fed it, naming her Candy. I have a lot of fond memories of this raccoon, so when my son wanted this raccoon, against better judgment and against the law of the land, I said okay. I did not realize that baby raccoons could have the rabies virus lying dormant in them for months before it would manifest. I knew in my heart that I was wrong to give him permission to keep this raccoon. But, like so many when we are out of the will of God, we justify ourselves. We stubbornly ignore the price that we will have to pay because of our rebellion and disobedience.

Daniel named his little raccoon Rascal. And he was a rascal because he was constantly getting into everything. A number of months went by and one night my son Daniel told me that he had a frightening dream. I should've known right then and there that we needed to get rid of this raccoon. He said in his dream, Rascal grew up and became big like a bear and then attacked and devoured him.

Some time went by and my son Daniel began to get sick, running a high fever. One morning, he came down telling me that something was majorly wrong with Rascal. He said that he was wobbling all over the place and was bumping into stuff. Immediately, the alarm bells went off. I asked him where his raccoon was. He informed me that Rascal was in his bedroom. Immediately I went upstairs to his room, opening his bedroom door. And their Rascal was acting extremely strange. He was bumping into everything and had spittle coming from his mouth.

Immediately, my heart was filled with great dread. I had grown up around wildlife and farm animals. I had run into animals with rabies before. No ifs, ands or buts, this raccoon had rabies. I immediately went to Danny asking him if the raccoon had bitten him or if he had gotten any of Rascal's saliva in his wounds? He showed me his hands where he had cuts on them, informing me that he had been letting rascal lick these wounds. He had even allowed rascal to lick his mouth.

Daniel did not look well and was running a high grade fever. He also informed me that he felt dizzy. I knew in my heart that we were in terrible trouble. I immediately called up the local forest ranger. They put me on the line with one of their personnel that had a lot of expertise in this area. When I informed him of what was going on, he asked me if I was aware of the fact that it was illegal to take in a wild raccoon. I told him I did know but that I had chosen to ignore the law.

He said that he would come immediately over to our house to examine this raccoon and if necessary to take it with him. I had placed Rascal in a cage making sure that I did not touch him. When the forest ranger arrived, I had the cage sitting in the driveway. He examined the raccoon without touching it. You could tell that he was quite concerned about the condition of this raccoon. He looked at me with deep regret informing me that in his opinion with 30 years' wildlife service experience, this raccoon definitely had rabies. He asked me if there was anyone who had been in contact with this raccoon with any symptoms of sickness. I informed him that for the last couple days my son Daniel had not been feeling well. As a matter of fact, he was quite sick. When I told him the symptoms that Daniel was experiencing, it was quite obvious the ranger was shaken and quite upset.

"GOD Healed Me HE Will Heal YOU"

He told me that anybody who had been in contact with this raccoon would have to receive shots. He went on to explain that from the description of what my son Daniel was going through and considering the length of his illness, it was too late for him! He literally told me that he felt from his experience that there was no hope for my son. He fully believed that my son would die from rabies. He loaded the raccoon up in the back of his truck, leaving me standing in my driveway weeping. He said that he would get back to me as soon as they had the test results and that I should get ready for state officials to descend upon myself, my family and our church.

I cannot express to you the hopelessness and despair that had struck my heart at that moment. Just earlier in the spring, our little girl Naomi had passed on to be with the Lord at 4 ½ years old. And now my second son Daniel was dying from rabies. Both of these situations could've been prevented.

Immediately, I gathered together my wife, my first son Michael, my third son Steven, and my daughter Stephanie. We all gathered around Daniel's bed and began to cry out to God. We wept, cried, and prayed crying out to God. I was repenting and asking God for mercy. Daniel, as he was lying on the bed running a high fever and almost delirious, informed me that he was barely able to hang on to consciousness. He knew in his heart, he said, that he was dying!

After everyone disbursed from his bed with great overwhelming sorrow, I went into our family room where we had a wood stove. I opened up the wood stove which still had a lot of cold ashes from the winter. Handful after handful of ashes I scooped out of the stove, pouring it over my head and saturating my body, with tears of repentance and sorrow running down my face. And then I lay in the ashes. The ashes got into my eyes, mouth and nose and into my lungs, making me quite sick. But I did not care, all that mattered was that God would have mercy on us and spare my son and all our loved ones from the rabies virus. As I lay on the floor in the ashes, crying out to God with all I had within me, one could hear the house was filled with weeping, crying and praying family members.

All night long I wept and prayed, (about 16 hours) asking God to please have mercy on my stupidity. To remove the rabies virus not only from my son, but from everyone else that had been in contact with this raccoon. I also asked God to remove the virus from Rascal as a sign that he had heard my prayers. I continued in this state of great agony and prayer until early in the morning when suddenly, the light of heaven shined upon my soul. Great peace that passes understanding overwhelmed me. I got up with victory in my heart.

I went upstairs to check on my son Daniel. When I walked into his bedroom, the presence of God was tangible. The fever had broken and he was resting peacefully. Our whole house was filled with the tangible presence of God. From that minute forward, he was completely healed. A couple of days later, I was contacted by the state informing me that, to their amazement, they could find nothing wrong with the raccoon. God had supernaturally removed the rabies virus not only from my son and those in contact with Rascal, but from the raccoon itself. Thank God that the Lord's mercy endures forever!

#35 Kidney Stones Completely Gone

A precious sister in Christ who attends the church I pastor ended up with kidney stones. She actually began attending our church when she was a young girl with her parents. From that time to now, she got married and had three daughters and a son. One day she began to experience extreme pain in the lower part of her body with nausea and vomiting. It became so painful that she decided she better get to the doctors real quick.

"GOD Healed Me HE Will Heal YOU"

She went through a serious of medical test, with the doctors discovering that she had many kidney stones. **What is a kidney stone?** A kidney stone is a solid piece of material that forms in a kidney when chemicals that are found in the urine become highly concentrated. A stone may stay in the kidney or travel down the urinary tract. A small stone may pass on its own, causing little or no pain. A larger stone may get stuck along the urinary tract and can block the flow of urine, causing severe pain or bleeding.

In Pam's situation the stones were so large that she could not pass them. Kidney stones are one of the most common disorders of the urinary tract. Each year in the United States, people make more than a million visits to their doctors, and more than 300,000 people go to emergency rooms for kidney stone problems.

Treatment for kidney stones usually depends on their size and what they are made of, as well as whether they are causing pain or obstructing the urinary tract. In Pam's situation the doctors informed her that the stones in her body were two large for her to pass, or for what they call shockwave treatment. In this particular procedure they use what they call a lithotripter to generate shock waves that pass through the person's body to break the kidney stones into smaller pieces to pass more readily through the urinary tract.

This treatment would not work for Pam though. The only other option they had was to literally go in with a long, tube like instrument with an eyepiece to find and retrieve the stone with a small basket or to break the stone up with laser energy. The urologist removes the stone or, if the stone is large, uses a flexible fiber attached to a laser generator to break the stone into smaller pieces that can pass out of the body in the urine.

When my wife and I went in to visit her as she laid in her hospital bed. She explained to us her situation, the diagnosis, and the treatment they were wanting to perform upon her. She told us that she really did not want to go through this procedure, and asked if we would ask God to remove the stones. **Absolutely** we told her that we were in complete agreement for a supernatural divine miracle to dissolve the stones. My wife put her hands upon Pam's abdomen, with me placing my hands upon my wife's hands. We commanded in the **name of Jesus Christ of Nazareth** for the stones to dissolve, to depart, to be gone. We commanded her body to be healed of all the damage the stones had caused. We commanded the pain and the discomfort to be gone in **Jesus name**. When we were finished praying we all began to praise God together thanking him for the healing that we had just spoke into existence. We left the hospital room agreeing, believing, and receiving by faith this miracle in **Jesus Name**.

From that moment forward Pam later informed us that all the pain had completely disappeared. As they were getting ready to perform the operation she told her doctors that she wanted them to double check once more before they carried out their procedures. She told them that after her pastor had prayed for her that all the pain and discomfort was gone. They reluctantly agreed with her request.

To their shock and amazement all the stones were gone. They examined her urine, but there was no stones to be located. They put her through other procedures and test, but every stone had just simply disappeared. Pam shared with them the fact that her pastor, his wife, and herself agreed together in Jesus name for the stones to be gone, and that God had answered our prayers. They were so upset about her sharing Christ that they quickly released her from the hospital with no comments. Christ is the same yesterday, today, and forever. If you ever did it once, he'll do it again.

#36 Bones snapping into place (2010)

One night as I was ministering at a service, there was an older lady standing in front of me who I had never seen before. I knew immediately by the spirit that she had a major bone disease. I informed her of such, and told her the spirit of the Lord told me he was going to touch her and make her whole. At the time I was not thinking with my rational mind, I was just flowing in the Holy Ghost.

By the spirit of the Lord I also told her that she should not be alarmed, because her bones would begin to snap and pop into place. The bones in her body would literally begin to go back to where they belonged supernaturally when I finished praying. I laid my hands on her in the name of Jesus Christ and spoke to the spirit of infirmity, commanding it to come out of her immediately. The spirit of God touched her in such a fashion that she began to slightly twist and turn as she fell under the power. We all stood there amazed as we heard and saw her body begin to come back in alignment. You could literally hear the bones popping as the spirit of Christ adjusted and healed her bone structure. We continued to minister to others as she lay on the floor having a divine chiropractor working on her.

She came back approximately a week later sharing with us the wonderful news that she was completely healed. All the signs of the bone disease (she gave us the technical term but I do not remember) were completely gone, and eradicated. Thank you father God for the wonderful works you do in the name of Your Son, Jesus Christ of Nazareth!

#37 Baby Healed from Incurable Affliction (2011)

My son Daniel and I Were ministering in a little country in South America, called Suriname. A Husband and Wife brought a little Child whose body was completely covered with some kind of rash. They told me that they had been too many doctors, but the doctors could not seem to clear this problem up. I laid hands on this little child and commanded this infirmity to go. Two days later they came back with their little child, and the rash was completely gone.

We saw many instant Healings in that country to the Glory of God. When I arrived back to our home church in Gettysburg Pennsylvania. I shared this miracle with our congregation.

There was a young man who was about 10 years old who came up for prayer. His arms were completely covered with poison ivy or oak. He asked me to pray for him. I laid my hands upon him and commanded the poison to leave his arms. When I was done praying, I turned away from him, getting ready to lay my hands on the next person. Immediately I felt somebody tapping me on the shoulder. I turned back to discover that it was this young man. He showed me his arms. All of the poison was instantly gone. I mean all of the poison, blisters, oozing sores were gone! Thank you JESUS!

#38 Three Amazing Testimonies (2012)

My name is Mary J. Rockwell. I would like to share three quick testimonies in which I saw God move in powerful ways in connection to Pastor Mike's prophecies:

Testimony 1: Years ago my mother was very sick and in the hospital in New York state. I had asked Pastor Mike to pray for me prior to leaving Maryland to go see her. He told me when I saw her I was to pray over her and say, "I command all tormenting mental spirits to leave her now in Jesus' name." Pastor Mike told me that the minute I spoke this word of authority that I was to clap my hands three times, and I was to say: **NOW!**

When I arrived at the hospital three of her doctors told me that she was going to die. My sister had called a pastor and began planning for her funeral. She had not eaten for days and had huge bags of fluid in the whites of her eyes and all over her face and didn't even look human. She was hooked up to IVs and monitors. I waited until only she and I were left in the room. I pulled the curtain around us, put my hands on her head and prayed just as the Lord told me to. I clapped my hands when I said, **"Now,"** and I felt a surge leave my hands and go into her body. The next morning I went in to see her. The IVs had been removed, she was eating, and all the pockets of fluid had disappeared from her face and eyes! The and the doctors were amazed. They released her that morning. She lived another three or four years.

#39 Testimony 2: I had fallen and broken both my wrists. The doctor had put a cast on one but I wouldn't let him cast the other. I went to Pastor Mike's home and he met me in the driveway. I asked him to pray for my healing, so he did. I went home and within a week I felt that my wrists were healed. I told the doctor either he remove the cast or I would have my husband cut it off. The doctor had told me I would have to keep it on for several weeks, but he reluctantly removed it. That same week I painted three ceilings by hand. The Lord had totally healed my wrists!

#40 Testimony 3: When my children were still in school, I went up to the altar for prayer. Pastor Mike prayed and said, "Your prayers have reached the very throne room of heaven. God said, " you will live to see all of your children serve the Lord. Your husband will be saved but he will be literally pulled out of the pit at the very end." My husband, at age seventy-two, contracted cancer from exposure to deadly chemicals while serving in the Marines in Vietnam. I had assumed that he knew the Lord. I prayed for him and said, "I could lay hands on you until you are bald, but you need to cry out to Jesus for yourself." He could not say the name, Jesus so I knew instantly that it was a demonic block.

I called a local pastor and was about to relate that to him when he told me that my husband's perception of salvation was wrong and he didn't believe he was really saved. He went to the hospital and prayed with him. My husband called me on the phone and said he had just received Jesus Christ as his Lord and Savior. His one regret was that he hadn't done enough for the Lord. The Lord had spoken to two young ladies who lived miles away from us to come and pray with him. When they came, my husband prayed for them and they wept and wept.

Three people who were there when Pastor Mike prayed for me called me on the phone and each of them reminded me of the prayer that Pastor Mike had prayed over me many years prior to that. Each of them inquired if my husband was saved and I told them it was just as Pastor Mike had prayed many years before. Since then, two of my four children are serving the Lord...two more to go!

CHAPTER NINE

#41 Healed from Gushing Bright Red Blood (2014)

With what I'm about to share with you, there is no pride, I am not boasting on me, but Jesus Christ. Since 1975 (when I was gloriously born again, and filled with Holy Ghost) every time I get attacked physically by a sickness, disease, or infirmity, I aggressively take a hold of God's promise: **by his stripes I am healed**, and that Christ has given me authority, power, and I can speak to the problem, the illness, or the disease, and commanded to go.

I DO NOT RUN TO THE DOCTORS BECAUSE I DO NOT NEED TO KNOW THEIR PROGNOSIS, MOST LIKELY IT WILL NOT BE GOOD ANYWAYS.

The answer to victory over sickness, disease, and afflictions is not by ignoring them, but by immediately rising up in the name of Jesus, and taking authority over the attack. NOW HERE'S THE STORY!

My wife and I arrived back from Israel on October 30th, 2014. While in Israel I had been experiencing some severe digestive problems. Specifically, when it came to bowel movements. When I got home back to Pennsylvania something was going on inside of me, and it just did not seem right. I sat down on the commode one day and perceiving something was really wrong. As I was having a bowel movement I began to gush bright red blood. When I was finished I stood up, turned around and looked down, and the commode was filled with blood.

Most people would have been immediately filled with fear,

called their family members, telling them what was happening, and rushed to the hospital, but this is not how I operate.

PLEASE PAY ATTENTION TO THE STEPS I TOOK TO BE HEALED!

The **1st** thing I did was examine my heart, making sure that there was no sin, or rebellion in my life, and I'm not talking about being sinless. We all have sin, because anything that is not of faith is sin. I am talking about open rebellion, disobedience, bitterness, hate, evil desires, sin in my heart, or life. In order to operate in authority, you must be submitted to the authority of God the Father, Christ, the Holy Ghost, and the Word!

The **2nd** thing I did was that I began to talk to God, thanking the Father for putting all of my sicknesses, diseases, and infirmities upon Jesus Christ, who took it all upon himself including our sins, and our iniquities.

The **3rd** thing I did was to **Speak Boldly** to the infirmity in my body, and the demonic powers. and commanding it, and them to go from my body in the Name of Jesus.

The **4th** thing I did was to now **Speak** to my body, my bowels, the intestines, the stomach, commanding them to be healed, and to be made whole. I commanded the blood to stop gushing.

The **5th** thing I did is I began to **rejoice and praise** God that I was healed, not that I was going to be healed!

The **6th** step is that I did not allow myself to be filled with fear, neither did I go around telling everybody, or anybody about the symptoms that were manifesting in my body.

The **7th** thing I did was to continue to thank God from that moment forward that I was HEALED until I saw, felt, and experienced its manifestation! I just kept on thanking God speaking to myself that **I WAS HEALED**.

"GOD Healed Me HE Will Heal YOU"

The **8th** thing I did was to **laugh out loud at the devil**, telling him that he is nothing but a liar, and that God, and his word is true. How long was it before you saw the manifestation of you healing? To tell you the truth, I do not remember.

Job 5:22 At destruction and famine thou shalt laugh: neither shalt thou be afraid of the beasts of the earth.

Job 8:21 Till he fill thy mouth with laughing, and thy lips with rejoicing.

The **9th** thing I do is that I endure, I stand upon Gods WORD! He that endures to the end will be saved. The word saved in the Greek is the word **SOZO**! This word means: 1), cured (1), ensure salvation (1), to get well (2), made...well (6), made well (5), preserved (1), recover (1), restore (1), save (36), saved (50), saves (1), saving (1). The person who holds onto faith when it comes to divine healing no matter what the circumstance, will be made whole.

The **10th** thing I do is that **I do not** let the symptoms of the sickness, affliction, infirmity control or dictate the course of my life! Now this attack was over a year ago, and I have no more blood in my bowel movements, feeling wonderful, and I am doing good in Jesus Christ.

#42 Pastor Healed Instantly of Cancer. (2013)

Pastor Healed of Cancer When She Was Called out with the Word of Knowledge! In Her Own Words: In the Month of February 2013, I was diagnosed with a large lesion in the upper left Chest area. Pastor mike I came to your fellowship, Jesus is Lord Ministries that Sunday Morning, I had The X-ray results from the study on my chair. I was praying that somehow that Father God would give ME an opportunity to share with you, and ask you to prayer for me.

Well do you know that during the time that you were delivering the message you stopped preaching, and asked me to stand to my feet because God had revealed to you exactly what I was dealing! This was without me telling you anything. You pointed directly to the Left side of my chest and said: I see a growth in your lungs. You then called me forward to be prayed for. You anointed my forehead with oil, and asked me to place my hand on my left chest, you began to pray for me, the power of God hit me, and we both jumped, and you said. "I'm waiting for the praise report" I was scheduled for a CT SCAN of my chest the follow Saturday.

The report from that study read: **"THERE IS NO LESION FOUND IN LEFT LUNG AREA"** I did return to Jesus is Lord Church and shared my miracle testimony with you, and the congregation. I want to thank you man of God for every time I've fellowship with your Precious Church family, I always get restored, refreshed and watered to overflowing. I've always know that this is a "Well of refreshing water for me". I'm grateful to Jesus for your prayers, intercession, loving kindness towards me, and Joy over flowing in my soul! Pastor Lauretta Melendez. Owings Mills, MD.

Pastor Mike's side of the story: as I was preaching the word of God, and looking over the congregation, something supernatural took place. As I was looking at Pastor Lauretta (by the way at the time I did not know in the natural she was a pastor - the Lord supernaturally told me that she was a pastor, which she confirmed later.) I had a very strong picture or image that floated up from my heart into my mind. I could literally see that there was a growth in her left lungs. As I saw this by the word of wisdom, and the gift of faith, I knew, that I knew God was going to healer this morning.

I stopped preaching, pointed my finger at her, and told her what the Lord said to me. She began to immediately rejoice, because that is exactly why she had come to our service. I called her up front, anointed her with oil, and laying my hands upon her. I cursed the growth in the name of Jesus, and commanded the growth and the cancer to be gone. Then I told her by the Holy Ghost that she needed to go back to the doctors, and get it confirmed. Praise God, I obeyed what the Lord said to me, she responded accordingly, and God healed her. Jesus Christ is the same yesterday today and forever!

#43 God Heals a Mafia Man's Eyes (2013)

I have a house where I take in and keep single men. Some of these men come from real rough backgrounds. I had one such gentleman that I was renting to who was quite large and intimidating. I would try to share Christ with him whenever the opportunity arrived, but he was so liberal in his thinking that it did not seem to be having any impact upon him. Everything I believe that is wrong, he proclaimed was right. And everything that I believe is right, he would argue against.

He informed me that in his past he had worked for the Mafia, and at one time he was what they called a THUMPER! I asked him what he meant by a thump-er? He said that he had never physically murdered anyone, but that they would send him to rough up people, you know thump them! I have no doubt at all that what he told me was true.

One day as I was at the house where I keep these men, I saw him standing in the main front room. He seemed quite upset and distressed. I asked him what was wrong. He informed me that he had just come from the doctors because he had been having terrible problems with his eyes. After the Doctor had conducted all of the test they came back with a very disturbing report. They informed him that he had an eye disease (long medical term) that was going to cause him to go blind.

At that moment the spirit of God rose up with in me as he told me this, and I proclaimed boldly that in the name of Jesus Christ he was not going to go blind. I told him: **close your eyes**! He said what? I said: **close your eyes**! He shut his eyes, and I took my two thumbs and laid them forcefully over his two eyelids. I declared: in the **name of Jesus Christ** you lying spirit of infirmity, come out of these eyes right now! **Be healed in Jesus name**! I then removed my thumbs from his eyelids, he looked at me with questioning eyes. I said to him: it's done! He said what? I said it is done. You are healed in the name of Jesus. He said: really? I said: yes Christ has made you whole. It seemed for a minute that tears formed in his eyes as I turned around and walked away.

Approximately a week later he showed up at a thrift store that we manage and operate. He walked into the store asking for Pastor Mike. They informed him that I was not there at the time. Tears were rolling down his face, and they asked him what they could do for him. He told them with great joy and excitement that he had gone back to the doctors, and that his eyes were completely healed. He started hugging the people that where they're running the store. This large ex-Mafia thumper gave his heart to Jesus Christ that day, and became a part of the church I pastor.

#44 God Instantly Heals Lady on the street (2015)

I had to get my snowplow one early morning, and then I took my lovely wife Kathleen out to eat to a local restaurant. As I was pulling in to the snow-covered parking lot, I noticed an older lady walking towards her car, holding her back with one hand moving very slow. It was obvious that she was full of pain, and being bent over was not helping her situation. At that very moment great compassion rose up in my heart for this precious lady. I knew the spirit of God was moving upon me to go and pray for this lady right then and there. I told my wife: the Lord wants me to pray for that little lady. I found a place to park my truck as fast as I could, hoping and praying that she would still be there for I could get to her. The parking lot was pretty crowded, plus many parking areas

"GOD Healed Me HE Will Heal YOU"

were filled with plowed snow so it took a little bit of time to find a parking space. I said to the Lord in my heart: God if you want me to pray for her, let her still be there after I park.

Sure enough, she was just sitting in her car, and not going anywhere. I walked up to her car, and rapped lightly on her window. She opened her door looking at me. I told her I was a local pastor, and that I had noticed that she was full of pain in her back. It was obvious that she was a little bit intimidated by my forwardness. She informed me that she had been everywhere trying to find help for the terrible pain in her back. She informed me that the disc in her have been ruptured.

During this time my wife walked up, and introduced herself. This particular lady's name was also Kathy, so this really helped to break the ice, because my wife's name is Kathee. I told her that I would love to pray for her if she would let me. She very timidly agreed. I asked her if I could hold her hand, and put my other hand on her back. She agreed to allow me to do this, and at the same time my wife reached in with one of her hands, and laid it gently on Kathy's back.

I took authority over this spirit of infirmity and pain, commanded it to go in the name of Jesus. I commanded her disc and her vertebrates to be healed, NOW IN JESUS NAME! As I prayed by the authority of Christ I did not lift my voice very loud, but spoke with authority almost in a whisper. When I finished praying I thank God for touching Kathy, and giving her a miracle. I immediately perceived in my heart that God had touched her, and given her an immediate physical touch!

I asked her to twist around in her car seat, and to check out her healing. A wonderful brilliant, shining smile came upon her face that was a look of complete and utter surprised. I asked her how her back was now. She told me with great joy on her face that the pain was completely gone. She had not been pain free for a long time.

Out of the blue she brought up another subject about a wonderful experience that she had just had two days ago. She informed me that her sister was a Christian, and had been praying for her. We spoke for a little while longer, and then said goodbye. She did ask me where I was a pastor? She informed us that she lived only about three miles away from where our church was. Then my wife and I walked into the restaurant not realizing that God was about to do another miracle for a very sick Catholic priest!

CHAPTER TEN
#45 CATHOLIC PRIEST DIVINELY TOUCHED
(2015)

After my wife and I had seen the spirit of God touch a precious older lady in the parking lot, we went into the restaurant and sat down to eat. As I sat there I perceive the spirit of God drawing my attention to an older man about six booths away from us. Now this older gentleman was dressed in the garb's of a Catholic priest. As I was looking at him with great compassion to my heart he looked back at me. I did not want to make it seem like I was staring at him so I turned away.

But before I knew it I was looking at him again, and then he was looking at me, and I was looking at him, and he was looking at me. This back and forth continued for about eight minutes. I finally told my wife that the Lord wanted me to go talk to this priest. I got up from our table and walked over to him. I began to make small talk with him simply trying to break the ice. It turned out that he was a teacher and a professor at Mount St. Mary's, in Maryland. I also discovered later that he was a famous author of books about Catholicism.

I introduced myself as a local pastor, and that is when he introduced himself. In the midst of talking to him he asked me if I knew the best way to the Turnpike. I gave him directions to the Turnpike, and help draw him a very simple map. After this conversation I went back to eat my meal with my wife. During mile whole meal my heart was being drawn towards him in compassion. I knew in my heart that there was something drastic going on with him, and he was full of fear. I also perceived by the spirit of the Lord that there was a spirit of death that was trying to come upon him. I said to the Lord: Father if you're not done, bring him to me. At that very moment he got up and began to walk towards us, and then he went past us. He stood close to the restaurants eating bar getting ready to leave.

Well, there was no way I was just gone to let him walk out of the restaurant without talking to him again. I spoke out to him saying: Sir something is going on in your body, what's wrong? He walked over to our table asking me how I knew this. I told him it was the spirit of God. I asked him what was wrong. He told me that he had blood clots in his body, in his right leg. The other day one of the blood clots broke free, and got to his lungs, but miraculously it was okay. He actually was headed to Pittsburgh in order to go to the hospital.

I asked him if I could pray for him, and he said I could! I took him boldly by his right hand, coming against these blood clots, and whatever was causing it. I commanded the spirit of infirmity to come out of him in the name of Jesus. Now of course the people that were in the restaurant were all watching, and hearing this transpire. I perceived in my heart that God had touched him as I prayed for him. When I was done praying he thanked me very much.(This opened the door to talk to another older couple who was sitting across from us.) This Catholic priest spoke a while to some of the workers of the restaurant who knew him. Once again he came over to our table and he thanked me with true sincerity for praying for him, and then he left. God still does miracles, we just have to BE willing and obedient. Yes, God loves and cares about Catholic priest.

#46 Black & Blue Foot Healed in 15 minutes (2015)

On a Wednesday night I preached a sermon on how you can BE healed without me. After the service brother Luke came up with brother Matt. He asked me to pray for his foot because he had messed it up at the potato farm that day. He took his shoe and sock off to show me the damage to his left foot. The left side of his foot

"GOD Healed Me HE Will Heal YOU"

was all black and blue, swollen and messed up. I told him to put his foot up on my knee as I was kneeling down in front of him. He asked me if I was sure that I wanted him to do this? I guess he asked me this because he was concerned about his foot might being stinky and dirty. I told him absolutely yes, he needed to put his foot up on my leg. He put his foot up on my leg where I was squatting in front of him. I laid my hands upon his yes, swollen, black and blue, dirty foot and stinking. Taking authority over this spirit of infirmity that was of afflicting his foot I said: in the Mighty Name of Jesus Christ of Nazareth I commanded the spirit of infirmity to come out of this foot right now. I command all of the swelling, the pain, the brokenness to be gone in the name of Jesus!

After I was done praying, he told me he was going to walk around a little bit. He left his sock and shoe off, walking through the sanctuary thanking God. I knew what he was doing! He was exercising his faith in Christ! After about 15 minutes I ended up in the back of the sanctuary talking to Matt and Luke about the things of the spirit. We were equally sharing back and forth about our love and excitement for Jesus, when out of the blue Luke said: look at my foot! We looked down, and to our wonderful joy, the swelling was completely gone, the black and blue this was also completely gone, and his foot was healed, and normal!

He informed us that he showed his mother his messed up foot before he came to church tonight. Now he was going to go back home, and show her what God had done! All praise and glory and honor be to Jesus Christ! God had wonderfully healed his back at one of our services not too long ago before this. Thank God his back is still healed, he showed us by touching his toes on Wednesday night! For a number of years he had experienced excruciating problems with his back, but even as the Lord had healed his back, he had now healed his foot.

#47 Woman healed who was bent over, blind, (2015)

A brother brought his wife who was legally blind, and crippled. On Sunday night the spirit of God had come upon his wife, and she ran for the 1st time in 3 years. Plus God had restored some of her eyesight. Last night (midweek service) when he brought her I could tell there was a drastic difference in her walking, in her countenance, even her eyes were not near as dim. She informed me that she did not even need her walking cane anymore. The night before she had come and was bent over, but tonight she was standing straight up.

I ministering on the subject of signs, wonders, and miracles last night. When I was done I called everybody up front. As I was ministering the word an praying for her, the Holy Ghost was all over her again. She was filled with great joy and began to bounce up and down, up and down, up and down! We didn't know exactly what was making her so excited, but maybe the Holy Ghost, but then she informed us that she could literally see the letters upon the wall which was probably 20 or 30 feet away from her. She was such a bubbly fountain of joy that some of us began to get drunk in the Holy Ghost. Once again I had her run by faith without any assistance. I did stand by her side a little, but she did wonderful. It's a progressive healing and she's getting better day by day.

As I anointed people's hands with oil there began to be an increase. The one precious sister who I'm sure is reading this really needs a miracle in her body from a car accident. I put a little bit of oil on her hand next to her thumbs, the next thing we knew as we were watching, both hands were covered with oil. We all stood there in amazement as God manifested his glory through the increase of oil. I gave her a prophetic word, that basically stated God was doing this to encourage her in her faith, and not to let go. That God was seeing her strong declaration that she was healed no matter how she felt. This Is the Faith that Pleases God!

"GOD Healed Me HE Will Heal YOU"

#48 Precious Elderly Saint Healed

The other day I had the privilege to go and pray for different people who had life-threatening sicknesses. I am believing that every one of them was touched by the Holy Ghost. I stopped at one house where last fall I had visited an older precious sister in the Lord. She had fluid on the heart, and congestive heart failure. When my wife and I laid hands upon her we knew that God had touched her. But we have not heard anything since then.

I brought her a number of my newer books because I know that she loves to read my testimonies. As I was talking to her she informed me with the most beautiful smile you have ever seen. Since you prayed for me I have not had any more problems whatsoever. She said: I do believe that God healed me!

Saints if we would only wake up and realize the authority that we have in Christ when we are completed submitted to him! I'm literally believing that every person I pray for will be healed! This may sound crazy, but I am getting myself ready to begin to visit hospitals. and hopefully pray for every sick person there.

Now I realize the medical personnel would not like this. But the Scripture says be as wise as the serpent as harmless as a dove. So I go in as one in authority by simply putting on a minister's collar and dress up looking almost like a Catholic priest. When I do this the doctors themselves seem to submit to my authority. I have gone into hospital rooms were doctors and nurses were, and kindly asked them to leave for I could minister to the person in the hospital bed. Surprisingly they bow their heads, walking out of the room.

One day I walked into a man's room who I did not know. I asked him what his problem was? He told me that his liver was completely shot, and that he was dying. I perceived in my heart that it was because of alcohol. I laid my hands on him, commanding in the name of Jesus for the spirit of infirmity to come out. Then I spoke in to him a brand-new liver, in the name of Jesus Christ of Nazareth! I do not yell or speak loud. I do not have to because I know my Authority! I do not pray long or tons of scriptures. The Word is already in my heart!

When I was done, I simply said goodbye, and out the door. I was to go see another sick person. It was 3 years later when we finally discovered what happened that day. One of the members of my congregation was down on the streets of Gettysburg witnessing. He ran into this particular gentleman, as he was sharing Christ. This particular man said: I know who your pastor is! The parishioner asked how this was? He said: 3 years ago I was dying with a bad liver. Your pastor walked in, laid his hands on me. And God gave me a brand-new liver!

Oh if only we would submit completely to King Jesus! Oh if only we would submit to his Lordship in every area! What miracles we would see wherever we go!!!

IMPORTANT INFORMATION: YOUR PREPARATION TO RECEIVE HEALING BEFORE YOU ARE PRAYED FOR & HANDS ARE LAID ON YOU! THIS WILL GREATLY INCREASE YOUR OPPORTUNITY TO BE HEALED!

#1 1st realize and boldly confess, **God wants to heal me** more than I want to be healed. It is God's will to heal me, no matter what I have done. It gives God great pleasure to heal people because he is a God of love and compassion.

#2 Go through the **4 Gospels** looking for every time Jesus healed people. Notice the Scriptures declare he healed them all. Every

"GOD Healed Me HE Will Heal YOU"

single person Jesus prayed for was healed. Most instantaneous, some progressive as they went, but they were healed.

#3 Recognize that **Jesus was the perfect will of the Father** manifested in the flesh. That everything Jesus did was based upon the fact that the father told him to do it. Hebrews says that Jesus Christ is the same yesterday today and forever. If he ever did it once, he will do it again.

#4 Get It Out Of Your Head, that you do not deserve to be healed. None of us deserve to be healed, it is God's mercy, love and kindness. Get it out of your head that the sickness you have is Paul's thorn in the flesh, or God trying to teach you something. These are all lies from the devil. Jesus Christ, God the Father, and the Holy Ghost are all eager and desiring to make you whole.

#5 Try to prepare your heart with **great faith and expectation** for what God is going to do through the whole day if possible. Get ready because God will not only heal that one particular problem you have, but he will be doing many other wonderful things for you in when you prayed for.

#6 Began to **boldly declared** to yourself (and others if you want to) that when hands are laid on me, Jesus Christ himself will touch my
sick disease body and I WILL BE MADE WHOLE! NO IFS, ANDS OR BUTS! I WILL BE MADE WHOLE! TODAY IS MY DAY TO BE HEALED, TO BE DELIVERED, TO BE SET FREE.

#7 BEGIN TO **PRAISE GOD RIGHT NOW**, THIS VERY MOMENT FOR YOUR HEALING, FOR YOUR DELIVERANCE, FOR YOUR FREEDOM! I AM EXCITED ABOUT WHAT WE'RE GOING TO SEE GOD DO IN YOU, TO YOU, AND EVEN THROUGH YOU!
Sincerely: Dr Michael H Yeager

ABOUT THE AUTHOR

Dr. Michael and Kathleen Yeager have served as pastors/apostles, missionaries, evangelists, broadcasters and authors for over four decades. They flow in the gifts of the Holy Spirit, teaching the Word of God with wonderful signs and miracles following in confirmation of God's Word. In 1983, they began Jesus is Lord Ministries International, Biglerville, PA 17307.

Websites Connected to Doc Yeager

www.docyeager.com

www.jilmi.org

www.wbntv.org

"GOD Healed Me HE Will Heal YOU"

Some of the Books Written by Doc Yeager:

"Living in the Realm of the Miraculous #1"

"I need God Cause I'm Stupid"

"The Miracles of Smith Wigglesworth"

"How Faith Comes 28 WAYS"

"Horrors of Hell, Splendors of Heaven"

"The Coming Great Awakening"

"Sinners In The Hands of an Angry GOD", (modernized)

"Brain Parasite Epidemic"

"My JOURNEY To HELL" - illustrated for teenagers

"Divine Revelation Of Jesus Christ"

"My Daily Meditations"

"Holy Bible of JESUS CHRIST"

"War In The Heavenlies - (Chronicles of Micah)"

"Living in the Realm of the Miraculous #2"

"My Legal Rights To Witness"

"Why We (MUST) Gather!- 30 Biblical Reasons"

"My Incredible, Supernatural, Divine Experiences"

"Living in the Realm of the Miraculous #3"

"How GOD Leads & Guides! - 20 Ways"

"Weapons Of Our Warfare"

"How You Can Be Healed"

Printed in Great Britain
by Amazon